Fury

By

H G Tudor

Fury

By

H G Tudor

Published by Insight Books

Introduction

Hello and welcome to Fury. What is fury? Fury is defined as a wild or violent anger. Since you are reading this book there is a possibility that you suffer from bouts of fury yourself although I suspect that this is unlikely. It is usually the case that those who suffer from some sort of affliction or disorder fail to recognise that they do. Awareness invariably comes from an external source. Even if they do, they invariably blame shift as they attempt to suggest that their shortcomings are the fault of someone who is entirely blameless. There usually is somebody who is at fault for these flaws. In fact, there are usually at least two. The person who created the problem and the person who does nothing about the issue are the people who are at fault. It is never the person who is the subject of the malign influence who is at fault, no matter how many times we may attempt ourselves to believe to the contrary. Accordingly, those who suffer from fury are unlikely to be reading this book.

It is far more likely that you are the victim of fury and in accordance with your reasoned approach to life you have decided to learn more about this subject with a view to understanding what is the source of the fury and why is it directed towards you? You are the one who has suffered the wild or violent anger and no doubt you have the battles scars to prove it. You no doubt will find an added resonance in a further explanation of what fury is. In Greek mythology, the Furies were three goddesses who executed the curses that had been pronounced upon criminals, tortured the guilty with strings of conscience and inflicted famines and pestilences. The product of those Furies was unpleasant in the extreme. Interesting though the Furies are, this book remains concerned with the concept of fury as a noun. In particular, its emphasis is on the fury that erupts from the narcissist. I am one of those individuals and if you are a regular reader (and if you are not, why not?) you will be familiar with my direct approach. I steer clear of the science that has evolved about me and revolves around me. Whilst there is much value in that, I find it tends to cloud the issue. If you want to read about what the perpetrator has to say about the topic of fury, then you want it in an uncluttered and to the point manner. You will gain most from this precious information being divested in this way. By embracing the no nonsense explanations and examples, drawn from my own experience and those who I have interacted with, then you will learn much about the way the narcissist uses fury to further his or her aims. I also acknowledge the assistance provided by Dr E and Dr O who have enabled me to achieve a greater awareness of the fury that courses through me. Through my sessions with them I have been able to understand why this fury exists, what its purpose is and why I use it? I have always had some understanding of the fury that I possess but I have been afforded a greater insight into its nature and effects through the assistance of the two doctors. They have helped me hone and polish my understanding.

We will be considering such questions as what is fury? How is this fury applicable to the narcissist? What purpose does fury serve for the narcissist? What does this mean for you? Why is the narcissist always in a state of fury? These and other questions will be addressed in my customary style. By reading this and considering the material contained herein you will gain a far better insight into the mind of a narcissist. You will also be aware that we are similar in the way we behave and think. This is especially true when it comes to the issue of fury. What you will read here will resonate with you in respect of your own situation. It may even prove to be the case that the methodology of rage that you recognise within these pages causes you to realise that you are in the grip of a narcissist, whereas before you were unaware that that was the case. The enlightenment can work in a number of ways.

Once armed with this information you can apply it to consider how you might look to escape the fury that is sent your way so often and if that is not possible then you may instead look at the way in which you can manage your situation to deal with the fury in a less damaging and more acceptable manner.

Read on and immerse yourself in the knowledge that follows about the narcissist and fury.

What is Fury?

Fury is the instrument of the narcissist. It is a tool that the narcissist deploys in furtherance of his or her aims. The narcissist's toolbox is a thing to behold. It contains many devices, objects and instruments that we deploy in order to secure our objectives. Other people may use these devices in a similar if diminished form but they will not be anywhere near as dangerous and effective as the ones that lurk in my toolkit. Some of these instruments are used to subjugate, others are deployed to control and yet again there are others that will be used for the purposes of manipulation. The placing of fury in this toolbox recognises its use to the narcissist as one of his prime instruments.

In determining what fury is, it will be instructive to start by considering what it is not. Fury is not anger. Anger is below fury on the scale of violent responses. Anger is a strong feeling of annoyance, displeasure or hostility. It is greater than vexation, it is something more than feeling cross and it is beyond exasperation. Notwithstanding this, it is less than fury. It does not contain the unbridled vitriol that is synonymous with fury. Nor does it contain the violent hostility that one finds with fury. What is most important to know about anger is that it is a normal emotion and thus by comparison, fury is an abnormal emotion, hence why fury sits in our toolkit. Anger is an intense emotional response that is normal in nature and arises as a consequence of real or perceived provocation. Anger in itself is neither good nor bad. It can be used for either purpose and it is down to the manner in which that particular person handles it. An individual may direct it into violence towards another person in order to protect him or herself from a threat. Alternatively, it may manifest in the destruction of property. You as a normal and empathic individual become angry. Indeed, as part of our mission to obtain fuel we strive to provoke anger in you, either through angry gestures or through angry words on your part. This provides us with fuel when you react in this emotional fashion. It is an acceptable and understandable response for an individual to become angry.

It is a normal response to a threat or harm. It also releases pressure that builds up inside a normal person. The expression of anger enables people to dissipate this pressure and thereafter feel spent but better for having been angry, as opposed to suppressing the sensation and allowing the pressure to build even further. Some normal people can only take a small amount of pressure before they blow a fuse whereas other people may be regarded as slow-burners who take a long time before they express anger. In either instance the response is an entirely normal one. People become angry for a host of different reasons, which may include: -

Facing a threat to themselves of their loved ones;

Losing out when money is involved;

Somebody contravenes a principle that is regarded as important to a person;

Being the subject of a verbal or physical assault;

Being treated unfairly but lacking the means to do anything about it;

Lacking control over something;

Being disappointed in themselves or in others;

Having one's self-esteem dented;

Having one's property mistreated

In all of these instances a normal response would be to become angry. Anger serves a useful response for an individual. It can result in the following: -

The activation of the fight or flight mechanism to deal with a threat to a person's well being or to the well being of other people;

A release mechanism for stress and pressure;

It enables people to move on from a situation;

The making of more optimistic risk assessments so that dangers appear diminished and certain actions seem less risky;

Motivation to achieve something worthwhile;

Motivation to work harder to overcome a problem;

Motivation to achieve a physical gain;

Moral indignation, which is harnessed as a force for good.

You may agree that anger certainly serves a purpose and concur that helpful and beneficial consequences can arise from this normal emotion. I should imagine that you will also venture to suggest that there is a downside to anger, that results in destructive behaviour and violence. That is not anger. That is fury. That is when something beyond anger is experienced and this fury is more prevalent amongst my kind for reasons, which I shall expand on below.

Interestingly, anger also results in a suspension of empathy by those who behave normally. The individual, through anger, becomes focussed on his or her own needs and requirements. This is not applicable to me. There is no empathy to suspend. That is why we do not deploy anger. We have no need of a device to suspend our empathy because we do not have any. This is a further reason why anger serves no actual purpose to us and why we must deploy fury instead. Anger is a normal reaction. We operate outside of the usual normative values. This normal anger serves certain purposes, which I have detailed above. None of those purposes are of any use to my kind and me. Anger can be regarded as a force for good. That is not something that we are interested in.

Fury is beyond anger. It is wrath, frenzy and savagery. Someone who is furious has gone the extra emotional mile. One might even consider it to be madness. The wild nature of fury causes it to surpass anger and fury is not to be found in the responses of the normal person. I will emphasise that point. You will not find fury as a response of a normal person. Anger? Yes. Fury? No. The deployment of fury is the hallmark of the abnormal. If fury were a normal reaction there would be chaos as explosions erupted everywhere. Most relationships would disintegrate, more people would be injured, and property broken and destroyed and the repercussions for society as a whole would be severe. The cost in terms of money, emotion and well-being would be enormous. Consider the number of times you have been angry. It has happened has it not? You will also be able to recall when your parents or at least one of them became angry, a friend, a stranger, a colleague or a partner. You have seen anger in everyone and that is because it is normal. They may have used that anger for some purpose, kept it in check or let it flow over them and dissipate with no consequence. For those of you have had an encounter with fury, you will also know it. It will have happened amongst fewer people than the categories that I have just mentioned. This is because the development of people has been such that fury cannot become the norm. If it does then society would begin to break down. You may have seen many instances of fury from one particular individual. That is because that person is not normal. They are the exception.

What does fury look like? Fury manifests in the following ways: -

Violence towards a person
Destruction of property
Excessive verbal assaults using profanity and insult, usually shouted
A sudden and swift reaction to a small problem
Accusations of friends and relatives going behind the aggressor's back, such accusations being based on perception rather than reality, driven by paranoia
Complete withdrawal, silent treatment, and sulkiness
A total lack of assistance, co-operation and willingness.

Most people regard fury as an explosive act of aggression but it also manifests in a cold, baleful fury, which sits churning away, boiling and seething behind an icy façade. These two types of rage are both present when our kind unleashes our fury. We can deploy both types with the same person, alternating between the two states as the fury remains but it is expressed in a different fashion. We can exhibit an explosive fury to one person and a cold, icy fury to another, sometimes in a matter of moments. This is achievable by us because it is not the fury that alters. That remains there at all times. It is the manner in which we choose to allow this fury to manifest.

This moves us onto another important point when it comes to the consideration of rage. Note how I referred to the fact that we **allow** our fury to manifest in different ways. The deployment of fury by our kind is a conscious decision. With explosive fury we may give you the impression that we have lost control. Certainly it is the case that we may do certain things within that explosive fury where we have lost control, for instance by lashing out at people physically, but you must realise that the use of fury has been a conscious decision on our part. Fury does not just happen with us. We choose to allow it to manifest because it serves a purpose to us (I expand on this further below). In the middle of our fury we appear much as if we are the overgrown babies having the mother of all temper tantrums. That is because we are lashing out with our hands, our tongues, kicking and stamping and creating a whirlwind around us. This behaviour may appear out of control but we are able to rein it in within an instant. We can douse the fury as quickly as it came. We can sublimate the fury to a cold fury if we choose and then back to an explosive one. This is because fury is one of our instruments.

We have learned to use fury as a tool to further our aims. Accordingly, this raises the question; how is fury applicable to the narcissist?

How is Fury Applicable to the Narcissist?

We have established that fury goes beyond the preserve of the normal. It is a reaction of those who are abnormal because fury is not a reaction that is proportionate or common. It is common to those who labour with what are considered disorders, but it is not common to the population as a whole. If you encounter someone who regularly unleashes fury, no matter how normal they may seem in every other facet of their life, the fact that this person engages in this behaviour denotes that he or she is not normal. It is important for you to grasp this point in terms of how you manage this fury (something I deal with later). You cannot make excuses for this person by suggesting that they are usually all right and it is just certain things that trigger this reaction. If this person were normal they would demonstrate anger as I have mentioned above. They would not bypass anger and unleash fury. Fury is therefore the preserve of the abnormal and this affects people other than narcissists. This publication is not focussed on the fury of those who are not narcissists. You need to know about whom fury applies to in respect of the narcissist in your life.

The narcissist has learned that fury is an instrument. The narcissist knows that this instrument can be wielded in two ways. Those ways are the subject of the following chapter. How has fury become applicable to the narcissist? Where did it come from? What was its source? How was it generated? I know that in my case my exposure and relationship with fury arose when I was young. I know that this is similar for many of my kind. In my situation I had two sources of fury that resulted in that very state of being becoming fused into my being. It was as if I had been imprinted with their fury so that it became part of me. It was however something more than just an imprint because I embraced that fury as well. I understood that fury was also method of controlling others. I actually realised that I could use fury as a method of control before I had the actual awareness of why my fury ignited and what purpose its manifestation served in a primary sense. The control that comes with fury is actually a secondary consideration, its main purpose is to protect us, but more on that later.

Remaining with the concept of control I observed this in action. As a quick learner and keen observer of the behaviour of others, my repeated exposure to this behaviour enabled me to learn from its manifestation and application, so that it became part of me. Fury became an instrument by which I could further my machinations, achieve my aims and secure what rightfully belonged to me.

The first fountain of fury was my mother. I do not remember the age I was when I first noticed how she unleashed her fury to get what she wanted. I know I was young, perhaps on the cusp of my secondary education. I never recall my childhood in a linear fashion, I am unsure as to why that should be the case. Instead I just recall specific events. They loom up out of the past, like figures appearing from the fog. The detail of those events is pin-sharp, the sound clear in my ears and the image crystal clear in my mind's eye. Yet, for all this clarity, I struggle to link the memory to those around it. It is as if each one is separate and distinct as if selected from elsewhere. At times I feel that a conveyor belt is always running through my mind and I am operating one of those claws you see at amusement arcades and fairgrounds. I am sure you know the type. You insert your money and you can then move a claw left and right, back and forth until you sense it is in the correct position to press the large red button and send the claw plummeting towards its target. Invariably, the claw impotently attempts to grab the stuffed toy or tantalisingly grips it and then begins to lift it upwards, your expectation rising until the weight of the toy causes it to slip from the quite clearly pre-loosened grip of the claw. Undeterred by this evident rigging of the machine, the player will funnel more money into the slot and try and try and try to capture the toy. I once watched a middle-aged man attempt to win a particular stuffed toy. It was a copy of a one-eyed creature currently popular in an animated feature film. He kept moving the claw, dropping it, missing the target, hitting the target but failing to grasp it, grasping it and moving it a few inches to the waiting maw of the prize chute. He kept feeding the beast that was the machine but no matter how hard he tried and no matter how much money he spent (I calculated he could have easily have bought three of the toys with the money he wasted feeding the machine) he did not win. Funds eventually exhausted he gave up and went elsewhere. Interestingly, I saw no young child with him who might have wanted the prize or at least egged him on to success. I wondered whom it might be for and as I watched him amble away it struck me how this machine represented two things material to my life. The first is where I began this recollection. The grabbing of the memory from a clutch of others is moved along this conveyor belt in my mind. Sometimes nothing is selected and on other occasions a memory is seized; only this is brought to the forefront of my mind. I embrace success as the isolated memory is recalled before it is discarded and the conveyor belt continues, parading various memories some of which might be grabbed and remembered, others destined to go round and round on this conveyor belt, never to invade my consciousness fully.

The second representation afforded by this so-called amusement is how alike it is to my quest for some sense of fulfilment. I channel the fuel from others in the same way as the man in my tale places coin after coin into the slot. This fuel allows me the power to function, the power to the crane and the claw, but what is the outcome? What is the consequence of all this effort and endeavour? Do I ever win the prize? Do I succeed or does success slip from my grasp every time, no matter how close the prize is to the chute?

Thus, from the depths of my childhood the occasional high definition memory is selected and brought to the fore. I recall several that involve my mother and her fury. I recall her as being a demanding person. She always reinforced to me how talented and special I was.

"A gift from God," she would say as she smoothed down my shirt or removed a piece of fluff from my shoulder.

"Always remember that HG, you were set on this earth to do great things and you must never shy away from your destiny. Ignore the clamour of the little people. Their petty jealousies are just that. Rise above them and spread your wings. Dominate and dazzle. Do you understand?"

I would nod in compliance (I knew the consequence of doing to the contrary) even though I did not, at least at first; understand the import of her words. That speech was said to me on many occasions. I do not need to send the claw looking for those memories because that speech has been etched across my mind and is indelible. She set the bar high and I was repeatedly reminded of my obligation. Any failure was met with swift punishment. Yes, she was demanding.

This condition of hers was not just aimed at me though. She was demanding of everyone. I used to see her fussing over the way that my siblings and I looked when a visitor came to the house. She ensured that the house was immaculate and she would berate the cleaners if she found anything out of place, unpolished or undusted. Everything had to be pristine. We could not run about the house (that was for outside) and our table manners were impeccable. Sit up, elbows off the table, chew quietly and never, ever speak with your mouth full. Of us all though I always thought that she made the most demands of my father and that was where I first observed her use of her fury.

I do not recall the exact details of what the event was but I remember over dinner my father explaining that he would not be able to attend a social event owing to a work commitment. There was a ball, which my parents attended on a regular basis. My mother sat on the organising committee and regarded it as a highlight of her social calendar. On this occasion, it appeared that it would not be possible to go. He explained it in a calm fashion. It was a matter of fact. He had no choice but to undertake the work and he explained, in what I thought was a reasoned fashion that he would of course attend the next time this event was organised but on this occasion he suggested that my mother go alone. I can still see in my mind's eye now how she reacted to my father declining this invitation. She did not even try to argue her case with him. She offered no protest or any attempt at persuading him. There was no raised voice or declaration of disappointment from her; she merely stared at my father as he continued to eat her meal. Her gaze was unwavering as her eyes narrowed and still she stared at him. I switched my view to my father but he was not meeting her gaze. He instead had taken a detailed interest in the steak that he was slowly cutting into. I watched as the serrated knife slid back and forth, cutting into the flesh of the meat until he severed a piece and he raised it to his mouth. Still he looked downwards, his mouth moving as he chewed and then the knife and fork shifted position slightly as he embarked on sawing away another piece to consume. I returned my eyes to my mother and still she stared at him, no, she glared at him. Her mouth was set tight, the veins in her neck prominent, her cheek bones, evident at most times, now looked as if they might burst through her skin, and such was the tightness by which they had become drawn across the bone beneath.

A few years after I first noticed this I watched a film called the Medusa Touch staring Richard Burton. It is an excellent film and a masterful performance from Burton. His character is able to bring about disaster through some form of telekinesis but invariably the catalyst for something terrible to happen would be the baleful stare he would subject his victims to. When I watched Burton carry out this stare I immediately recalled the look that my mother gave my father than evening (and on subsequent occasions). It was as if she was willing something awful to befall my father as a consequence of his refusal to attend the social event.

Sat at that table she glared at him and then we all jumped as the glass around which she had gripped her hand shattered, spilling red wine on to the tablecloth. My mother let the shards of glass fall and still maintaining her stare stood up. My father had jumped as we all had when the glass broke. We all turned in the direction of the noise. He did not. He remained fascinated by his steak. As the first droplets of blood rose in the gash in her hand my mother walked away from the table. My sister pushed back her chair and made to pursue my mother.

"Rachael," said my father, "leave her be, there is a good girl."

My sister hesitated, looking towards the archway through which my mother had walked and then sat down. My mother did not re-appear to mop up the spilt wine as she might ordinarily have done and instead the purple stain slowly spread across the tablecloth as my father finally looked up and began to ask us about our days at school.

For approximately a week after this incident my mother did not speak to my father. He would try and engage with her at our evening meal but she never answered him, instead turning to speak to one of us instead. I saw my younger brother, when asked a question glance nervously towards my father before answering, unsure as to whether he ought to answer her. I watched, as my father would follow after my mother as she walked through the house.

"Please, enough of this, let's just talk about it."
"This really should not happen in front of the children you know, they will be worried."
"This is ridiculous, when are you going to grow up?"
"Look I am sorry but is this really necessary?"
"Come on, I have said I am sorry until I am blue in the face. What do I have to do to get you to speak to me again?"

He issued those pleas and others, as he would traipse behind her, trying to block her progress as she marched haughtily from room to room. Gone was the normal glide that she adopted when she walked around our house. Normally she moved with elegance and a refinement. Not now. Now she strode, arms pumping and feet stamping the floor. I could feel the fury she exhibited travel into and along the floor.

This impasse between my parents went on all week. My two younger siblings were unnerved by it and worried that our parents would split up. I would hear them whispering about it and casting furtive glances towards where my mother would be sat, the aura of fury emanating from her as my father would pander to her, bringing cups of tea that would go undrunk and magazines whose pages would not be turned. Whilst my two younger siblings were worried, my elder brother was unmoved and even dismissive.

"Oh she always does this when she has not got her way, she will calm down eventually, always does."

He would make such a remark and then go back to whichever book was occupying him at the time or the painting of his metal miniatures for his role playing games. He was not bothered by it at all. It was evident he had seen it many times.

The younger two fretted, my elder sibling dismissed it and I was fascinated by it. How long could she keep this up for? Was it easy not speaking to someone for such a long period of time? Why was she speaking to other people and not him? How could she flick between being pleasant on the telephone to her friends and then ignoring him when he asked who was it who had telephoned? How was she managing to keep this up? I would secrete myself in a position where I was largely unseen (one became adept at doing that in our household) but it enabled me to observe this enthralling dynamic between the two of them.

Just over a week had passed and I had been dropped off by a friend's father following football practice. I kicked off the dirt from my boots before sitting on the doorstep and pulling the boots from my feet before putting them in my bag and entering the house. I crossed through the porch and then into the entrance hall. I made my way upstairs to take a shower when I could hear my mother and father talking in their bedroom. It was a lively and pleasant conversation and they were both laughing. I was surprised to hear my father's voice, as I had understood that this was the evening when he had to undertake some work for a client. I wondered what had happened.

Once showered and dressed I made my way to their bedroom and lightly tapped on the door.

"Come in HG," said my father pleasantly. He was adjusting his bow tie in the mirror, the freshly applied cologne dominating the air. I could not see my mother but I could hear her moving around in the en suite bathroom.

"How was football?" he asked.

"Oh it was fine thanks, where are you going?"

"To the ball," he answered. I nodded and then walked out of the bedroom smiling to myself as I realised what had happened. He had relented. Her period of freezing him out had caused him to change his mind and instead he was now attending the ball with her.

After this incident I paid careful attention to my mother and she harnessed this fury, this cold, ice-like fury to her advantage. I learned that that was what was coursing through her veins when she would sit ram-rod stiff, her face a mask of taunt annoyance, the lips pursed and those blue eyes glinting with malice. There was no explosion, no eruption and no raised voice but it was fury and from that first time I saw it in her and the effect that it had, I recognised it time and time again. I purposefully watched for it and when it came I made sure I studied carefully how she directed that icy fury. Not once did she allow it to escape as shouting or the hurling of crockery about the dining room. She kept a lid on the explosive nature of her fury and channelled it as an icy fury.

I witnessed on one occasion how she had a disagreement with the planning committee of a local charity about the method of applying funds for a conservation project. That night when she returned from the meeting I saw the mask of fury had been placed on her face once again and the sharp, clipped tone she adopted when speaking on the telephone to the relevant members of the committee told me all that I needed to know. She responded by withdrawing her support to the charity on the basis of a "difference of principle". This in turn led to the business in which my father was a majority shareholder removing its sponsorship of the programme and a close friend of my mother's who was the banqueting manageress at the most prestigious hotel in the locality removing its offer of allowing the charity access to its banqueting hall for free. Within four days of the removal of her co-operation, which was how she channelled her fury, the committee had "looked again" at the proposal and decided to support my mother's methodology. In an instant of the telephone call arriving to inform my mother of this, the sharp tone melted away, the ice thawed and she was back on the committee, resuming the sponsorship deal and securing the banqueting hall once again.

When my younger brother was not admitted to the first eleven of the cricket team, the wife of the selector was excluded from various social events. She was ignored in the street when she sought to bid my mother good day and found that she was suddenly barred from the village's two pubs. My brother was made captain the following week.

If my mother did not get her way, if she was unable to achieve the very things she knew that were hers as of right and if she was not afforded the recognition her various good works merited the fury would be ignited. People would be ignored, favours withdrawn, blockades erected, assistance removed and a steely demeanour exhibited towards the transgressor. Nobody was immune to this manifestation of her cold fury. Friends, family, the vicar, shopkeepers, publicans, police officers and acquaintances all knew the force of the famous Tudor ice storm. It worked. My goodness it worked and most of all it worked on my father who found himself the recipient of so many bouts of silent treatment he might have wondered if he had fallen deaf. Every time he pleaded and begged for a different outcome but my mother was a glacier. A vast sheet of ice that could not be moved by anyone else and was moving at its own pace and in its own direction and if you resisted you would be eroded and subsumed into this edifice. I marvelled at this power. How magnificent was she that she was able to have a grown, principled man such as my father almost on his knees begging her to stop the silence and speak to him. This was a man who ruled the roost at a private school as headmaster, but he was relegated to the role of a first year infant when it came to dealing with my mother and her icy fury.

Through years of observing her use of this cold fury, I learned how effective and powerful it was. The ability to cause others to do your bidding and all it took was withdrawal and silence. I was impressed. I understood her fury too as I had begun to experience it also. What I felt was surely the same as what she felt, I could see it in the ice that formed in those bright blue eyes and I knew that I had what she had. I had been blessed with her gift and thus when the fury filled my mind, seared through my blood and consumed me I knew how to channel it. I had the knowledge through the experience of seeing a master artisan at work and I too was able to apply it as I saw fit to further my own agenda with the generous application of sulking, silent treatment, withdrawal and the removal of co-operation and assistance. In the way I saw it coming with my mother, others began to recognise that 'look' so that they shrunk away in anticipation of the hurt that would surely follow. I marvelled at my newfound power and was content to wield it to ensure that my way was the only way.

Thus, this is how I learned to use the fury in a cold and calculated manner. Where did the ignited fury itself come from? I will tell you all about that in the next chapter. You will also need to understand that we have a simmering fury that is always there and an ignited fury which is what causes a problem for those who cross us. At present I must continue with explaining how the fury became applicable to me. I have explained the origins of how I learned to use fury as a device of ice from my mother. There is a second source from which I learned too. This was my Uncle Peter, my mother's brother. He was five years older than her and in her eyes he could do no wrong, he was brilliant and an over achiever. She would regularly regale us with tales of Uncle Peter's brilliant accomplishments over dinner. I could sense, as I grew older, that my father was sceptical about much of the content of these professed achievements but he knew that there was nothing to be gained, at least for him, in challenging the basis of these stories. He would listen, no doubt having heard the anecdote on several previous occasions and nod supportively, although his eyes belied a weariness with hearing about how Peter did this and Peter did that and 'isn't Uncle Peter just marvellous?'

My uncle Peter had continued the family business that had been established by my mother and his grandparents. They had established a chocolate factory, or a confectioner's as my mother preferred to call it. This was the source of my mother and Uncle Peter's wealth, which had been passed down to them. Now it was Peter's turn to stand at the helm of the factory and steer it as it tackled the rigours of the late twentieth century.

"Everybody loves chocolate and everybody loves me," was Uncle Peter's repeated refrain. Uncle Peter was a tall man, statuesque and he dominated conversations. He knew about anything and everything and loved nothing more than to hold court amongst a group of people as they latched onto his every word, none more so than my mother who looked at him with utter adoration at her big brother. Uncle Peter would arrive at a family event and nothing was allowed to start without him. He would stroll into our house, the pub, and the restaurant or wherever it might be with his wife and my four cousins trailing behind him. Uncle Peter never entered a room; it gave way under the force of his charisma and had little choice but to admit him. Even now he has retained his handsome features and is always immaculately attired, something I have taken my own sartorial cues from. Heads turned whenever Uncle Peter arrived, ears pricked up and eyes widened as he dominated the room, doling out his products to grateful recipients.

"Here we are Rachael, try this new chocolate, I know you will love it," he would declare as he thrust a bar into her outstretched hand. "Sister, have a taste of this," he would announce breaking a chunk of some exotically named bar and pushing the piece into her mouth, his fingertips lingering on her lips, or was it the other way around? "The Belgians do something similar, but mine is better," he would add as my mother marvelled at the taste.

"What do you think of this?" he would ask as he pressed a new confection into the hands of another guest and he would stand over them until they had opened the wrapping, tasted the product and declared their delight. He would nod in confirmation at their correct answer. Uncle Peter and his chocolate were the two things that always had to be addressed. He was no Willy Wonka however. He had no interest in whether people were actually happy about his products, he just wanted people to tell him how marvellous they were and thus how fantastic he was. How do I know this? I shall tell you. This came from my first experience of his fury. In fact, I was able to observe two separate appearances of his fury in one afternoon. Just like his sister, my mother, the arrival of Uncle Peter's fury proved instructive.

It was a Saturday in June and a splendid, hot day. The sky was cornflower blue with not a cloud to be had and my father had got his timing right again as he had organised a barbecue for family and friends. Naturally, my Uncle Peter and his friends had been invited to attend and with the sun high in the sky, he arrived with a box of chocolate under his arm. He emerged onto the rear lawn where a number of guests had already arrived. My father was stood talking to a friend as he tended to the barbecue and my mother trilled to everyone that Uncle Peter had arrived. Heads turned and children headed towards him eager to receive his bounty. He handed out the bars of chocolate as my mother greeted him and my father waved across from behind the rising smoke from the barbecue. Uncle Peter had unwrapped one of the bars as my mother introduced him to a neighbour, Cliff I think it was.

"Here try this, we are going to launch this next month, tell me what you think," said Peter as he snapped a piece of the dark chocolate from the rest of the bar and thrust it towards Cliff. He moved his head back, slightly alarmed at the aggressive offering of the chocolate.

"No thank you, I am enjoying this," replied Cliff lifting his plate on which a couple of pieces of barbecued meat nestled with a corn on the cob.

"Oh go on Cliff, it really is the best," enthused my mother.

"No offence but it isn't really the weather for chocolate," protested Cliff. Uncle Peter did not move the chocolate but held it in front of Cliff before nudging it towards him again.

"Try it," said Uncle Peter. Cliff looked to my mother who hovered nearby and she gave a nod.

"Well, er, if you insist," answered Cliff and picked the lump of chocolate from Peter's fingers and popped it in his mouth. He sucked on it and then bit down and began to chew the chocolate. Uncle Peter stood waiting, ignoring the children dancing at his feet as Cliff ate the piece that had been proffered.

"What do you think?" asked Uncle Peter.

"I am not keen," answered Cliff, "it is too rich for my liking; I prefer the chocolate that you normally get in the shops."

"Are you joking?" asked Uncle Peter.

"No. Why? I don't like it."

"Are you some kind of fucking idiot?" roared Uncle Peter.

"I beg your pardon?"

"Oh you will beg alright, you moron. That chocolate "in the shops" is made from shitty ingredients, you ball sucking bastard, it is made with palm oil, but this, " growled Peter as he thrust the box of chocolate bars upwards, "is a premium product, not that I would expect a wanker like you to realise. Jesus, I don't know why I bother with arseholes like you, you have no idea."

I noticed my mother had taken a step back. She made no attempt to stop her brother.

Uncle Peter took a step forwards and knocked Cliff's plate from his hand sending his meal into the air. There was a gasp from those assembled.

"Let me ask you this Cliff. What have you ever created? Eh? Fuck all I bet. You probably push paper from one side of the desk to the other don't you? I bet you do not wake up and feel supercharged because you are going to create something. Well I do and I will tell you why I do, because I have balls you pathetic excuse for a human being."

Uncle Peter's voice had risen as he bawled into Cliff's face. He grabbed his crotch to emphasise his point.

"I get sick to the back teeth of you safety kids who never try anything new. You just sit and moan and want the same old thing. Wake up!" he yelled again making Cliff jump.

"Really there is no need for this," replied Cliff a tremor in his voice.

"There's every need. I get up and every day I am thinking about how I can make my products better. How can I ensure that we stay ahead of the competition and keep our customers happy? How do I ensure that this premium quality outsells its inferior rivals? Then I come here and some moron like you tells me you do not like it. You know jack shit you arsehole, jack shit I tell you. Jesus, I have a good mind to bend you over and shove this entire box up your arse but why should I waste such a good product on a pleb like you eh?"

"I am not standing for this," answered Cliff and he walked away, making for the garden gate.

"Yes, that's right, run away you pissy knickered wanker," bellowed my uncle as he snapped another piece of chocolate from the bar that he still held. I stood watching as he had unleashed this tirade against Cliff. My uncle was easily four inches taller and many pounds heavier and would have sent Cliff flying if he had struck him. My uncle's eyes bulged and swivelled in their sockets as his face had turned red. His shoulders were hunched and yet despite this he looked larger as if the fury that was clearly raging through him had caused him to grow. His chest rose and fell with the urgent breaths that he was taking. His feet were clamped to the ground so that when he spoke he swayed back and forward, his shouted words ringing all around the garden. I watched and waited for the clubbed fist to slam into Cliff's face but he managed to remove himself before that came and instead scurried away, fresh insults following him. I was not shocked. I was more amused.

"Here, taste this," demanded Uncle Peter as he rammed the chunk of chocolate towards another neighbour who had been stood next to Cliff. Without speaking, this neighbour took the chocolate and quickly ate it.

Well?" snapped Peter.

"It is excellent, rich and smooth, I am sure it will do well," replied the neighbour, his words spilling out fast and low.

"Damn right it is," answered Uncle Peter as his voice dropped several decibels. He pulled at his collar and then resumed passing out the bars of chocolate to the children who had skulked nearby, having retreated as he exploded with his fury. The storm had passed. The smiling, benevolent Uncle Peter had returned with my mother flapping about him, mopping the beads of sweat from his brow. I continued to watch as he moved about everyone and I mean everyone on that lawn, handing them pieces of chocolate and scrutinising them as they tasted it, each person nodding and affirming how good it was. He did not stop as he patrolled the barbecue, eliciting praise and admiration from everyone there, including me. I was amazed at how he had been able to summon up such fury and direct it towards Cliff, his barking voice making those around him jump and then afterwards the way everyone agreed with him. It was powerful and I wanted it.

It did not take too long for Uncle Peter to demonstrate more of his fury. He had taken up a position on the patio, securing a prime seat (which was usually my father's seat) so that he was afforded the sun whilst being able to regale a group of people who he had gathered about him as he spoke about one of his business trips. It was somewhere in China or similar I think. I was to one side of the lawn talking with one of my friends as we sat on the grass, enjoying the heat of the sun and the cold of the cola we drank. Uncle Peter's voice rose above the general murmur of chatter in the rear garden, occasional laughter and noises of surprise and delight puncturing his tale. He had sent my sister to fill his plate again as he stood up and removed his white linen jacket and placing it over the back of his chair. He sat down and adjusted the linen trousers and pulled at his gingham shirt before taking a drink of his beer and continuing with his story. As my sister walked across the lawn she tripped as she reached the patio and two sausages flew from the plate that she was carrying for Uncle Peter. One hit the floor and the other struck Uncle Peter's right trouser leg leaving a dirty smear of grease and blackened flesh across it.

"For fuck's sake," erupted Uncle Peter as he slammed his glass down.

"Sorry Uncle Peter," said my sister as she picked herself from the floor and rubbed at her scathed knee.

"Sorry's no good, do you see what you have done?" he bellowed and rose to his feet, pointing a finger at the smudge on his pants. In one movement he snatched up my sister and placed her across the large metal table that was on the patio. He lifted her skirt and exposed her knicker-covered bottom. With an open hand he spanked her several times as she began to scream and kick her legs.

"This will teach you to be more careful," he shouted as her howling cries rang out. He then roughly replaced her on the patio, her skirt falling across the bright red hand marks he had left on her bottom and the top of her legs. Tears spilled down her face as my sister raced inside. She did not go to my mother who was sat nearby, her face oddly devoid of expression. I twisted my head and looked to my father who was still stood by the barbecue. He seemed to be frozen to the spot.

"Jesus, has she any idea how much these pants cost?" seethed Uncle Peter.

"I am sure it will wash out," soothed a lady nearby.

"You don't wash these you fool," hissed Uncle Peter at her, "God's teeth, I am surrounded by incompetence here. Come on Sandra," he said to his wide, "we are leaving."

At this my mother broke her reverie and implored Peter to stay. She fussed over him, taking him inside to see if she could attend to the mark on his trousers as the rest of the guests exchanged glances and muttered to one another, disapproval evident in their gestures. My father left his station at the barbecue and made his way inside, no doubt heading to check on my sister.

"Your uncle is a maniac," commented my friend, Tony.

"I know, "I answered, "Cool isn't he?"

Thus my second tutor in the application of fury had made himself known with two eruptions in the course of one afternoon. I was taken aback, not in fear or revulsion, but rather in admiration at how Uncle Peter had managed to summon this all-consuming fury and unleashed it left, right and centre. He had people frightened of him and eager to escape him, as Cliff had done, yet everyone else had soon flocked to him once more, ready to listen to his stories, as if they wanted to be associated with this powerful man. Nobody reprimanded my uncle for his treatment of Cliff, who was a long-standing neighbour, not my father, none of the other neighbours and certainly not my mother. He had reacted with violence towards my sister over her error. Served her right really. She ought to have got it right and not dropped his meal and marked his trousers. She only had herself to blame. She had brought it on herself. Uncle Peter was right to be annoyed with the incompetence that he had witnessed.

After that afternoon I saw other instances of the sudden eruptions which Uncle Peter engaged in.

One Christmas he flew off the handle at my Auntie Sandra for forgetting to make the brandy sauce (even though she had made everything else for a sumptuous dinner). Uncle Peter tore a strip off her in front of everyone else and had her in tears as he sat fuming. As if to compound the omission, my mother then went and made some to placate him.

I was once in a car when he was cut up by another driver. I was a teenager at this point and Uncle Peter in his large Mercedes hit the roof at the driving of the other man. Swearing and waving his hands about like a madman, he deviated from our route and followed the man to a supermarket carpark where he punched the man to the floor before kicking his brake light in and returned to his car.

"That's how you handle arseholes that cannot drive HG my son," he commented as he slid back into the driver's seat, breathless from the exertion of the brief fight.

On another occasion I saw yet more evidence of Uncle Peter's rage and the way that he used it in an explosive fashion. He had acquired a rock factory to make the teeth rotting substance that is so beloved at coastal holiday resorts. I was undertaking some work experience over the summer holidays when I was fifteen years old. There was plenty of work and it was certainly an experience. I had been around the chocolate factory on several occasions. It was the jewel in the crown of Uncle Peter's expanding confectionery empire. The factory was set in landscaped grounds, the delicious scent of chocolate wafting across as one neared the factory. The front of the operation was housed in an elegant country house, so meetings took place in drawing rooms with high vaulted ceilings. There were lots of mirrors throughout the house, which always stuck in my mind. To the rear of the house was the expansive factory which was pristine inside, well-maintained and a real showcase. There were no oompah-loompahs but the employees worked hard for my uncle.

By contrast the rock factory which Uncle Peter had acquired was on an industrial estate tucked away and whilst not dilapidated it was nowhere near on the scale of the chocolate factory. The interior was functional and drab. I can still picture it all now along with the smell of sugar and glucose. I was involved in the creation of the mixture which was used for the centre of the rock. This involved several buckets of glucose that were obtained from a huge vat on one side of the factory. This was poured into what was basically a large cauldron. Sugar was added, with preservative, colouring and so on. I would stand adding the ingredients and stirring it as a woman stood next to me picking the wasps out of the mix. I kid you not.

The majority of the workforce, namely those engaged in the production of the rock and its wrapping thereafter were straight from Brave New World. Most of them were epsilon semi-morons. I remember that there was one fellow who if you bent over near him he would kick you up the backside and accuse you of stealing his pay packet, even when it was not pay day. Another woman would put 'The Laughing Policeman' on over the public address system and then jump up on one of slabs that were used for cooling the rock and then placing the wrapped products on it. She would hitch up her coat and skirt and sing along, dancing manically. They were all perfectly polite to me, but then as the owner's nephew, they knew they had to be. Uncle Peter gave me a lift to the factory on my first day of working there.

"This will wake you up me laddo," he smiled as we pulled into the car park, "it is a dump but a profitable one. You would not believe the money it makes and now I have it, how much more it will generate. This will give you a taste of what life is like at the sharp end and will be all the incentive you will need to make sure you study hard and go to university. These idiots should have tried harder at school or they would not be here."

He was right. I hated it. I was stood on my feet for long periods, my fingers and hands became blistered from wrapping pieces of cellophane around the hardened stick of rock and the rock lollipops.

The radio that blared all day long was only ever on one station. This was not too bad if there was popular song that you liked as one was guaranteed to hear it at least four times a day. If however there was one which you did not, as there was when I was there, a Michael Jackson ballad, it was torture, especially since the girl who I worked opposite loved Michael Jackson and would screech along each time the song came on. I soon learned which jobs to avoid and managed to persuade my co-workers to do those jobs and I in return promised I would make mention of how hard they worked to my uncle since pay review time was around the corner. I found their gratitude and thanks edifying. I never said anything to Uncle Peter. He would have crucified me for even mentioning these people to him.

Occasionally Uncle Peter would prowl around the manufacturing base watching what was going on. At first people spoke to him as the new owner until he unleashed his fury at them for having the temerity to speak to him. He would find a fault, any fault, with the way someone was wrapping the rock, or stacking a pallet, or making up the cardboard boxes, or adding too much glucose, or not shutting the glucose tank tap off properly and enter into one of his furies. I saw two men burst into tears, one woman get sacked on the spot and one fellow receive a black eye for arguing back, as a consequence of these tirades. It was not long before Uncle Peter's inspections resulted in silent obedience as he stalked the aisles, the work force keeping their heads down and showing that they were working hard. Productivity increased or as Uncle Peter explained after my six week stint,

"These fuckers now know their place and it is doing what I want."
I was in awe of the man. He was a pioneer, an achiever and his weapon of choice was explosive fury. I saw how he wielded this, how he harnessed his inner fury and let it vent in the world. I saw him shove people, bark in their faces, smash pallets up, drag people about and have them trembling as his fury poured over them. If it was not done correctly he would erupt. They soon learned and so did I. Power flowed from this explosive fury and I wanted it.

Thus I was tutored well in the application of fury. First by mother who was an expert in the art of ice-cold fury and also by my uncle who was the walking equivalent of TNT. I saw what their fury could do and I knew that that was what I would do with the fury that raged inside of me.

I learned that fury gave you control. It gave you power over people and made them do what you want. It made them scared of you, eager to please you, admire you and fawn over you. This fury could be used as both shield and sword. It was used to deflect and shut-out and it was used to coerce and cajole. I studied extensively by watching my two relatives and from time to time as I grew and developed I would recognise it in others. I became an expert at discerning those who used anger and the true specialists who utilised fury. I belonged to the latter group and realised that by harnessing my fury in either a cold or explosive way, I would achieve recognition, fear, admiration and power. This was the way forward.

Having learned therefore some use of my fury (but not all of the uses, more to come on that) the question becomes as follows; what ignites the fury?

What Ignites the Fury?

Fury is ever present. I explain below why that is the case. It is always there churning away. In order for fury to be deployed it must be ignited. What is it that causes this fury to become ignited? What triggers it? What causes it to manifest so it that can be used to direct an explosive eruption at someone or shut them out with an ice cold front?

At first I always knew the fury was there. It is an ever present sensation and something which I explore in greater detail in a later chapter. I learned from the two tutors I have described above how I could unleash the fury in two different but effective ways. The fury is always there but it has to be ignited. There has to be a flashpoint which causes the fury to escalate so that it can be directed as I have explained. If there is no ignition the fury would just remain, churning away, burning and boiling but ultimately serving no purpose. It has been generated but before it can be applied either as an explosion or as a cold front, it must be ignited. For a long time I found the fury would ignite readily enough and thus I was able to use it to control and yield the results I wanted but I was never fully aware of what was actually happening when this ignition took place. What caused the ignition?

It was around the age of twenty when I was at university that I recall what prompted the ignition of my fury. I realised at that time that something would cause the fury inside me to ignite and it is in my later years, with the assistance of Dr E and Dr O that I have been able to look back on this period of my life and establish that that was the time when I gained an awareness of what it was that caused my fury to ignite.

Through my discussions with Dr E and Dr O I have understood that my best recollection of the earliest ignition of my fury took place during my interview for a place at university. It was early December in the late 1980s and time had just crossed the threshold into early evening. It was already dark and several lamps lit up the atmospheric study in which Professor Z and a Professor T sat. Professor Z was sat at an impressive desk. Professor T was sat off to one side on a window seat and I did not even see him until Professor Z introduced him. Neither moved towards me, necessitating a short walk on my part to where each man was positioned to shake their hands in greeting. They were letting me know that I had walked into their lair.

I had spent the afternoon reading and reviewing, analysing and dissecting a case study that had been provided to a number of us who were being interviewed for a prospective place at this college of a prestigious university. The case study considered the question of causation. It revolved around a Jehovah's Witness who had been subjected to a violent albeit not fatal assault with a knife. She required a blood transfusion and in accordance with her beliefs she refused it and died. This raised the question of what had caused her death. Was it the wound that arose from the plunging of the knife into her stomach or was it her refusal to accept the necessary blood transfusion? I entered the study and was invited to sit. After some introductory chit chat we began to discuss the case. Professor Z posed a question and I answered. He then pulled my answer apart as I fought to respond. He would advance a new proposition and I would seek to counter his proposal before he tore that to shreds also. It was akin to watching two duelling swordsmen but I was being backed repeatedly towards the edge of the cliff. He asked a question, I answered it and he then attacked my answer. I gamely fought back but each time he moved the goalposts and blew apart my reasoning. It was not the case that he was cleverer than me. Not at all. He just had the advantage of knowing the case study inside out and I knew that he will have been through this routine hundreds of time. He knew every permutation, every likely answer that a candidate would give and he had the advantage of preparedness. Professor T said nothing. He remained impassive sat just off to my right and slightly behind me so this meant I had to keep twisting in my chair to address both academics. I am sure they had created this situation on purpose. I took solace in knowing it was an unequal battlefield that we stood upon. What I did not like was the way he criticised my answers.

Professor Z was easily six foot three inches in height. He was lean and his silver hair was back combed adding another inch to his height. It also revealed his prominent forehead behind which lurked his formidable mind. His gaze was steady over the half-moon spectacles that he wore and each sentence he spoke was delivered in his strange accent but in a level manner. I later learned he was a Transylvanian Jew so that at least explained his accent to me. His delivery was steady, devoid of emotion and was provided in such a way that whatever he said was given the veneer of being an unarguable fact. His voice did not rise or lower but stayed at the same pitch, with the same inflection and it was this emotionless, relentless destruction of my arguments with a clinical, cold criticism that I now know proved to be the ignition for my fury.

As each sentence landed I felt myself growing weaker. I was gaining nothing from this man and all he was doing was landing body blow after body blow against me. He no doubt delighted in his intellectual rigour as it battered mine but he was unaware of the damage that he was inflicting on me inside. I wanted to flee the interview but that would be admitting defeat and would also put an end to my aspiration to be admitted to this particular college. I could not leave even though that was all I wanted to do. I could not stand this assault for much longer as I felt myself shrinking and withering.

I wanted to lash out in order to prompt a reaction from Professor Z. I needed to get those eyebrows to rise, the implacable expression to alter, his voice to shift in some way but by attacking him I was sufficiently aware that this was likely to extinguish my admission prospects. I needed help from some quarter and then realised that Professor T had played no part in my interview so far. What was his role? Was he there just to listen and allow Professor Z to flex his mighty intellectual muscles and make me wither? The incessant and calm criticism of my arguments ignited the fury and I whipped around in my chair to face Professor T.

"I am of the view that the point I have just made is one based on a solid foundation, wouldn't you agree Professor T?"

I snapped at him and I saw him jerk his head at being addressed directly. He smiled and I saw that it was smile of congratulations.

"Absolutely Mr Tudor, it is a point which carries considerable force and might I add," he responded and his agreement and appreciation made me feel a surge of power inside. I had harnessed Professor T as an ally. That was his reason for being in the interview. He would offer nothing until the candidate had engaged him as an ally. His impressive mind, allied with his mastering of this particular brief enabled him to lock horns with Professor Z. Each time Professor Z sought to knock down my argument and thus ignite my fury, I directed this fury to jolt Professor T into life. Professor Z would drive an icy question at me, I would reply and then as the fury would race through me, I would not direct it against Professor Z but would use it aggressively to prod Professor T into helping me. I could not belittle Professor Z, that would defeat my application, but I could harness Professor T as my shield. His assistance and appreciative affirmations of my comments gave me enough fuel to protect my wounded self from Professor Z.

I was admitted to the college. I learned that one of the reasons I had been selected for admission had been as a consequence of my aggressive and bullish responses in my interview. I did not, as I would with the later use of my fury, stray into the realm of destruction and belittlement, but I now realise that this was the first time I realised what caused my fury to ignite. It was criticism. My skirmishes with Professor Z did not end at that interview. He was one of my tutors and he clearly recalled that afternoon in early

December as he revelled in trying to defeat me during our tutorials. He applied that same emotionless and clinical dissection of my papers, theories and arguments and each time it would ignite my fury. I would often sit in silence and refuse to contribute further to the discussion. It brought no admonishment from Professor Z but rather he appeared to respect the fact that I had said my piece and was sticking by it and needed to say no more. He would turn and toy with another student in his study as I remained silent; glowering at him as I applied the lessons I had learned from my mother.

Looking back I realise that my application of my ignited fury was not always as precise and effective as I would have liked. Indeed, it bore little resemblance to the efficient and effective unleashing of my fury that I engage in now. I was still learning my craft and understanding the ways in which my fury could be applied. What I had learned, albeit unconsciously back then and only brought to the fore more recently by the good doctors, was what provided the flashpoint for my fury. The fury that was always there but needed something to ignite it for it to be used in an effective fashion. The method of ignition was criticism.

How Does Criticism Affect Us?

When you or for that matter anybody criticises us then you are negating our splendour. You are pouring scorn on our magnificence. We detest criticism. We despise it almost (though not quite) as much as if we are not given fuel through indifference or inattention. Criticism cuts through our construct and drives a poisoned point into our midst. It burns, it tears and it hurts. The wound you create in our construct causes us great pain indeed. It is important that you do not confuse criticism with anger, hatred or name-calling on your part. If you unleash anger towards me then, be it through a gesture or words then that is fuel. It has no consequence to me other than to give me the very thing that I crave. Expressing your hatred towards me only does a similar thing. Yet, should you disagree with me then you are failing to acknowledge how I am right. You are denying that I am superior to you. Level a criticism at me and you land a sledge-hammer blow against my construct, shattering the shards and breaking its segments apart.

The criticism must however be delivered in an even and unemotional method. Your disagreement must manifest in a calm and measured manner. There are two parts to this equation:-

1.   Criticism or disagreement; and
2.   The method of delivery

In the same way that our fuel is generated by a combination of the proximity of supply and the method of delivery, so it is the case that the wounding potential to our construct can only be generated by a combination of these two elements in the correct fashion.

1.   If you shout and bawl at me telling me that you hate me and I am a bastard, there is no criticism (it is just name-calling) and there is no unemotional delivery. All you are doing in this circumstance is providing me with fuel. Keep going. I will suck it up all day.

2.   If you tell me that I cannot cook a decent meal as you sob over the burnt pudding that I place before you this will not breach the construct either. You have criticised me but you have negated its impact because you have wrapped it up in emotion. It is like trying to stab me with a dagger that is still in its sheath.

3.   If you stand before me and coolly remark that I am not witty or intelligent than you have breached the construct and struck through it. You have criticised me and done so without the muffling effect of emotion.

When you land these blows against my construct you are generating a risk that the whole edifice will come tumbling down with the consequences that I have described above. This cannot and must not happen. Even if the construct does not collapse, the fact that you have blown away part of it means that there is less that I can reflect.

"You are useless in the sack," immediately wounds me and strips away that segment of the construct which portrays that I am an Olympian between the sheets.

"That painting you have done is not very good," wrenches away the section which demonstrates that I am a credible artist.

In addition, as you land these strikes against my construct you are increasing the risk that the creature that lurks will be able to make itself heard and seen through the gaps that appear. You are encouraging it to try and escape and this increases the possibility of our destruction. I cannot allow the construct to remain damaged in this way. You have smashed a hole in it through your criticism and I must address this damage promptly and effectively. I have three choices available to me.

On the one hand, I can seek to shield myself from your criticism and repair the construct. One way of doing this is to withdraw from the situation. This will shield me from further criticism and allow me time to repair the wound without it becoming worse. As the sting of your criticism recedes then the wound closes over.

The second option is to shield myself and repair the wound in a situation where withdrawal is not a viable option.

The third option is to use the ignited fury as a weapon. To go on the attack and rapidly gather negative fuel which repairs the wound and also by using fury as a weapon I increase my superiority so that your criticism loses its effect rapidly. Before I explain each of these three methods of protecting myself against your wounding criticism it is necessary to understand the dynamic of the construct, power, ignited fury and fuel.

1. The construct has two purposes. It is used to gather more fuel and it acts as a prison;
2. Keeping the construct in place requires power. When I am powerful I can maintain the construct. If power weakens, the construct begins to erode and may collapse.
3. Power is usually obtained from fuel.
4. Fuel is gathered either in a positive or a negative sense from emotional reactions as I explain in detail in my book **Fuel.**
5. Ignited fury can be used as a weapon (to gather more fuel) or as a shield (by channelling the ignited fuel into power)
6. Where the ignited fuel is converted into power, this depletes the fury temporarily.
7. The newly created power (from ignited fuel) is then depleted as it creates a shield and repairs the wound.
8. Both the ignited fury and power have been depleted. The shield is intact and the wound repaired. Fuel is needed immediately to replenish the power.
9. The fury will replenish over time (by reason of the way we perceive the world) and becomes ready to ignite once more and used either as a weapon or a shield.
10. Fuel is at the heart of everything. This is why it is so important. This is why we need it so much

You need to keep the above ten points in mind as I take you through how ignited fury is used as both a shield and a weapon and in doing so you will understand how and why we act as we do.

The Application of Fury: Withdrawal

Before I discuss the use of ignited fury as a weapon or as a shield, we need to consider how in the light of criticism we may decide to withdraw.

In some instances we may disengage for fear of further criticism. This is one option that is open to us and occasionally we take it. We may find ourselves in a situation where this first blow is not a terrible one but we sense that more injury awaits us. In such circumstances we will look to disengage and retreat so that we can address the wound promptly. Our fury will have been ignited by your criticism. We disengage and do so for the following reasons:-

1. This immediately stops further wounding from additional criticism;

2. The act of withdrawal acts as the shield. We do not need to use our ignited fury to convert to power to shield us. Thus we save energy;

3. In our bolthole we can then use our ignited fuel to convert into power to close the wound. We feel powerful by channelling our fury into this and accordingly this reduces the effect of your criticism until it no longer wounds us.

4. Our ignited fuel has been depleted by conversion into power. It will replenish over time.

5. Our power has been depleted by its use to close the wound. It needs to be replaced with fuel but we did not need to use up

too much power to close the wound and therefore the need for fuel is not pressing.

Accordingly, you may observe that in instances where you have criticised the narcissist in your life that he or she disappears and remains away from a period of time. This is to create a shielding effect from your criticism, use converted ignited fuel to power the repair of the wound, dole out some absent silent treatment to you and then look for fuel from a different source as well. If we know these is another source of fuel that we can engage quickly in order to replenish our power then we will take that option. The appliance that provides this fuel must not be the individual who has caused us damage through his or her criticism of us. That is too great a risk. There may be further criticism and this will cause greater damage. Instead, we will remove ourselves and seek out the alternative source of fuel so we can restore the power that has been used to patch up the superficial wound you inflicted on us through your criticism.

You should be aware that when faced with criticism that withdrawal is always considered. We will always look to do this first because we hate being criticised and we want to get away from the source of the criticism and give us time to repair our wound. In the less disciplined members of our kind this manifests itself in a propensity to flounce. A criticism is levelled at that person and it wounds, it burns and it pains. They may not even consider the other options available to them and instead just remove themselves from the situation. I exert sufficient control to ascertain whether removal is the best option. Often it is not and will have additional consequences such as ridicule or condemnation from those who hold some authority (whether I like it or not) in my environment. Others of our kind are not necessarily blessed with the awareness or control to discipline their use of withdrawal. That is why you will see someone drive away from being "criticised" by a traffic police officer. The police officer pulls the narcissist over and tells him he was speeding. The narcissist regards this as a criticism of his driving skills, the criticism wounds and without regard for the consequences of driving away from a police officer, the narcissist does just that. Alternatively, they may storm out of a meeting where they have had their idea criticised or their contribution criticised and their exit occurs irrespective of disciplinary action that may take place. Where you witness a narcissist who disappears at the first criticism of them you are dealing with someone who must do that in order to protect themselves but you are dealing with someone who lacks the discipline to apply their ignited fury as a shield or a weapon. They must get away and thus shield themselves from further attack. They must get away and use their ignited fury to repair the damage and they do this irrespective of what else might follow from their rapid exit.

The more sophisticated and disciplined of our kind use our ignited fury as either a shield or as a weapon, dependent on the scenario.

The Application of Fury: The Shield

The second application for the use of fury once it has been ignited is in a situation where withdrawal cannot take place or it is gauged to be unviable, but a shield is required to prevent further criticism and the wound must be repaired.

I have explained in **Fuel** how we create a construct. This is a necessary device to ensure our existence and our survival. Without this construct we are not able to garner additional fuel and nor are we able to exist because we become subsumed by the creature that lurks beneath. The construct is created from the shards, fragments, sections and pieces that we appropriate from other people. You may describe it as cloak, a mask or a tower. Whatever description is used, this edifice is constructed from all of those traits and characteristics from others that we regard as desirable. By obtaining these segments we can then use them for ourselves and in turn attract people to us. This means that more people will flock to us and thus we have more appliances available to provide us with fuel.

The fuel provides us with power to keep the construct in place. When we are powerful the construct is strong and impregnable. The glittering and shining shards reflect what we want you to see and thus we are able to attract you. It is also ensures that the construct performs its second role, that of a prison. I experience considerable discomfort in acknowledging the existence of the creature that lurks below. If you wish to read more about what that thing is, I suggest you read **Fuel.** For now, it is sufficient to explain that this creature must not be allowed to escape. It has to remain trapped by the construct. Accordingly, the construct is extremely important to us. It provides us with a magnet for fuel and acts a prison. The maintenance of this construct is paramount and without it we are lost. We have no means by which we can attract sufficient fuel, this means that our power wanes and the consequence of this is that creature is freed and we are consigned to oblivion.

For the most part, the construct is only vulnerable to the attacks from within of the creature as it tries to claw its way out. So long as our power remains strong we can hold the construct in place, and repair any damage that this beast causes. Unfortunately there is another way in which the construct can be damaged. This is caused by you, or her or him. The next door neighbour might do it; a school teacher could have this effect, a friend or a colleague too. In fact, the very people that supply us with fuel are the ones that can also damage our construct. The circumstances in which this can happen are very precise. As I have explained above by reference to my early days at university, it is criticism or disagreement that are the loathsome weapons that punch holes in our construct and it is their method of delivery that is crucial to whether this criticism or disagreement breaches our construct.

Criticism or disagreement do two things:-

1. They wound us; and
2. They provide the flashpoint, the ignition for our fury

I have explained above that withdrawal may take place. Sometimes for physical reasons withdrawal just cannot take place. In other instances, it is a step we could take but the more disciplined and astute of our kind realise that withdrawal could have other unwanted consequences and therefore it has to be dismissed as an option to address the criticism that we have suffered.

If withdrawal is not an option then we must still repair the construct straight away. There is no hope to retreat and re-evaluate. We may be unable to latch onto another source of fuel to allow the repair to take place or if there is fuel available there is not enough of it. We must repair the damage immediately before the repercussions are felt. To do this promptly and effectively we need power. Using power to effect the shield and repair means using up fuel. If the power becomes depleted and there is no fuel to replenish it then the whole edifice of the construct will come crashing down and we will be destroyed.

The use of ignited fury as a shield occurs in situations where:-

1. We cannot or choose not to withdraw;
2. We cannot or choose not to use the ignited fury as a weapon;
3. There is insufficient fuel to convert to power to effect the shield and the necessary repair of the wound

In this scenario we can, for a limited period, convert our ignited fury into power rather than use fuel to do so. There is always a simmering fury within us (for reasons which I shall expand on below) but to bring it to the fore and use it to repair and shield means that we must convert the ignited fury into power. The ignited fury that we create is immediately used as a shield. The ignited fury creates the power that we need to repair the construct. It also and in the moment this is of greater importance, enables us to drive back the person that has criticised us. It shields us from further criticism whilst our construct is repaired.

How does this happen? Let me provide you with a couple of examples.

I am criticised by a current intimate partner at a social gathering. Many of those attending are admirers of mine and form part of my coterie. Indeed there are a few lieutenants in attendance also. I have carefully cultivated an image of success and likeability in order to gather positive fuel from various sources. This veneer of charm and good nature lends credibility to my later observations that you are the crazy one when I begin my devaluation of you once you let me down and fail to be the efficient fuel providing appliance I require. Accordingly, maintaining this façade to these people is of paramount importance. Your criticism is delivered in a calm fashion and immediately wounds me. My simmering fury is ignited. Much as I would like to tear a strip off you, berate you and shout at you, hurl glasses and plates around in order to garner an emotional reaction from you, I know that such a display would alarm and shock my admirers. Moreover, it would send my carefully crafted façade crashing to the ground. I am aware enough of my need for this façade and the effect upon it of an aggressive use of the ignited fury. I choose not therefore to utilise an aggressive manifestation. Of course, the criticism still wounds and has punched a hole in my construct. I must stop this attack and its wounding effect.

I could withdraw from the social occasion but that would seem out of place. Certainly it is not beyond the realms of possibility and I am sure you have witnessed occasions when the narcissist in your life has flounced out of some gathering. He or she will have done that to escape any further wounding criticism. I decide that withdrawal is not an appropriate reaction but I must repair the construct and I must do so fast otherwise the lurking creature will escape and make its presence felt.

Accordingly,

1. I choose not to withdraw to avoid denting my façade;
2. I cannot use the ignited fury as a weapon otherwise it will destroy my façade;
3. You have minimised the fuel available to me through your action so it will not generate sufficient power that is needed to protect me from further criticism and to repair the existing wound.

I am wounded by your criticism and my fury is ignited. I channel this into power which is then used to shield me from any further criticism (I feel more powerful by using this ignited fury so I am above your criticism) and this converted ignited fury makes me feel powerful so that the effect of your criticism is vastly diminished.

I utilise my ignited fury as a shield. I say nothing to you and show no reaction to what has been said. As I do this, I am channelling my fury into power and my power is being used instead to repair the construct. I use this power to effect the repair, shielding me from the wounding effects of the criticism but as I do this my fuel is being used up and reduced. I convert the ignited fury to make me feel powerful and then use this power to both shield me and to extinguish the effect of your criticism (and thus in effect repair it). I now have reduced my ignited fury (which will replenish over time, but must be given chance to do so) and reduced my power. I need more power to keep the construct in place and therefore I need more fuel.

With the criticism dealt with through the shield and repair I now turn my attention to gathering more fuel. I will then engage in flirtation with an attractive female in order to gather positive fuel from her and hopefully a negative emotional reaction from you when you see me shamelessly flirting with her. You may not react though and thus I will need to keep finding fuel from other sources to replenish the use of my power to repair the construct and shield me.

Accordingly, it is normally the case that fuel provides me with power in order to keep the construct in place. If I am wounded by criticism I may use fuel generated by the fury to override it (I discuss this below in using fury as a weapon) but I may not be in a position to deploy this particular method. I cannot use fury to gather additional fuel to repair the wound because of the situation. There may not be any way of gathering fuel even if fury could be unleashed in such a way. There may not be enough fuel available even if there is some to hand. Without the necessary fuel to power the repair of the construct I face destruction. I am thus forced to channel the fury into power instead. There is no aggressive reaction and instead I sublimate the fury into the power which repairs the wound. This depletes the power and if this power becomes exhausted the whole construct will topple. Accordingly, I will need to find additional fuel to replace the power that has been used up. I cannot use fury to gather this fuel for two reasons:-

1. The situation has not allowed me to do so ; and
2. In any event the fury has been channelled into power instead

The fury becomes the power. The power repairs the wound. This has reduced the fury (when it is used to create power) and has reduced the power (when it has been used to repair and shield). With both fury and power depleted, I have repaired the wound and shielded myself from further injury but I am now at risk of the whole construct come tumbling down because my power (which is used to hold it in place) has been reduced. I must find additional fuel, most likely from positive sources which will then replenish my power and allow the fury to grow naturally once again. Now you see why our desperation for affirmation and admiration is such when faced with criticism to which we cannot react with fury as a weapon.

That is why when you criticise us and we cannot react with fury as a weapon (or that does not work) we seek positive fuel from other sources as quickly as we can. We repair the wound, using fury driven power and now need fuel to replace the spent power.

Thus the situation has necessitated action to prevent the destruction of my construct, an act which has been commenced by your criticism of me. My fury was ignited and I chose to use it to shield me, drawing on my power and depleting my fuel, in order to prevent the construct from being destroyed. My public façade is maintained and I have both evaded destruction and preserved the edifice that I have created for my later manipulations.

A further example presents itself from the world of work. Let us consider a situation where I have made an internal presentation to my boss, a number of peers and also a group of my subordinates. I am pleased with the presentation but my boss levels a criticism at me. He delivers it to me in straight tones and it wounds me immediately. The effect is compounded because this criticism is taking place in front of an audience. I am tempted to walk out and thus withdraw from further injury but I have sufficient awareness to realise that such a course of action would prompt ridicule (which would generate further criticism of me) and may even result in censure from my boss. I am not in a position to allow my ignited fury to manifest in an aggressive fashion, not if I want to keep my job and therefore I need to shield myself. I reply politely and calmly despite the fury that is raging within. I have to use my existing power to repair the wound and channel the fury in that manner by using it to shield me as the repair can be undertaken. Of course my fuel is being depleted and accordingly I turn to a subordinate who I know will support me (for reasons which do not need to be expanded on here) and thus his admiring words provide me with some fuel to allow me to regain a degree of power. If the power that is being used to conduct the repair was all used up, with no fuel to replenish it, then nothing would hold the construct in place and I would be doomed. Accordingly, when I channel the fury into power and then use that power up, I need additional fuel to replace the power that is being used up. In this instance I have:-

1. Had my fury ignited by the criticism;
2. Evaluated that I cannot withdraw;
3. Evaluated that I cannot use fury as a weapon;
4. Opted to create a shield and repair the wound;
5. Channelled the ignited fury into power. By feeling powerful I feel shielded from further criticism;
6. Grown in power and thus this diminished the effect of the criticism (allowing the wound to be repaired)
7. My ignited fury has been reduced and will replenish over time;
8. My power has been used to shield and repair and must be replaced;
9. I have gathered fuel to replace some of the used up power and thus keep the construct in place. I will need more fuel and quickly.

This is exhausting and intensive work and this is why we react in such a manner when criticised.

Accordingly, where you have criticised a narcissist who cannot or will not withdraw and cannot or will not use ignited fury as a weapon, you will force him or her to use his ignited fury for the purposes of shielding him or herself and repairing their injury. This in situ scenario drains both our ignited fury and power so the hunt for fuel becomes all the more pressing. You will witness the narcissist in this instance immediately look for fuel from various sources. Often it is not possible to draw fuel from you straight away (because we risk further criticism and this then becomes a self-defeating step) so we have to extract our fuel from sources separate to you as our primary source of fuel. This means you will often find us going to a mistress, heading out with our friends or flirting with other people as we seek fuel. We may turn on other family members to create the negative fuel to increase our power, or lash out at colleagues or even strangers. Without being privy to this knowledge you might think that we have just walked off in a strop and begun to abuse other people for no reason. There is a very clear reason. You have forced us to use our ignited fury for power and both have been used up. We need to allow our fury to replenish and we need fuel and we need it fast.

The Application of Ignited Fury: The Weapon

I have always known that I am superior to many people. I also knew that people recognised my brilliance and that was why they wanted to be around me, to show their admiration of me and to want to bask in my reflected glory. I have learned that some people do need to be reminded of my stature and station above them. My position above them is in the natural order of things. It is this knowledge that I am entitled to walk this earth and do what I must do because I am superior that enables me to keep the construct in place. I am powerful and therefore I have the power to maintain the construct. Doubtless you are reading this and thinking this is arrogant and I have a high opinion of myself. Yes I do have such an opinion but it is based on fact. I am a high achiever and I wield power over people in a number of ways, all reinforced and assisted by my manipulative gifts. Accordingly, my opinion of myself is founded on something solid.

Unfortunately there are those that seek to divest me of my power. These people apparently revel in trying to hurt me and make me feel weak. These people are clearly envious of my position and rather than accept that this is the proper order of things they spend their time looking to bring me down. It is cowardly and unpleasant. Naturally, the way in which they go about this attempt to dethrone me is to criticise me. These people level unfounded criticisms against me and do so in a cold and clinical fashion. It is hateful behaviour and I despise them for it. These criticisms wound me and drive holes into the construct risking the unleashing of the creature that lurks within. In order to remedy this unfair and unnecessary attack I will go on the offensive. My simmering fury has been ignited by this criticism and on this occasion it does not manifest as a protective shield but rather as a weapon used to strike out at those who seek to do me harm.

The manifestation as a weapon can take two forms. Firstly it can be an explosion of rage akin to those I learned from my Uncle Peter. A scorching, furious rage which is total and vicious. To you it seems to come from nowhere. I have repeatedly heard those who have been on the receiving end comment that it seemed to erupt from nothing. Naturally, it is typical of them to try and trivialise my hurt by describing it as nothing. How would you feel if someone was trying to destroy you? Pretty furious I should imagine. Why should I then be any different? I have learned from the good doctors that the nature of some of the criticisms that ignite my fury would be regarded as trivial or amazingly not even criticisms at all when looked at through your worldview. I understand that the good doctors are only relaying to me what they believe to be the truth and I suppose that this is the case when looked at through the lens of your worldview. To me, however, I do not understand how these criticisms can be seen as trivial or non-existent. I see them for what they are; calculated attacks designed to destroy me. I have now understood that in your reality you may regard them as nothing to be overly upset about. In an odd way I envy the fact that you are able to brush them aside so readily. I am not able to do so. It is evident that this is because we are created differently. You are designed and created to see the good in everyone, to care and to nurture. I must be wary of the intentions of others for my role as a pioneer and leader engenders jealousy and envy. This results in people saying and doing things which are calculated to topple me, to bring me down and cause me to crumble to dust. Yes, I have heard many people say to me,

"Where on earth did that come from, all I did was express an opinion about your car/clothes/kitchen/suggestion/observation." Those flippant comments twist the critical knife further into me. Not only have you criticised me you now regard my reaction as misplaced or unacceptable. I find such an attitude reprehensible. You have done something which strikes at my very core and you expect me to act as if nothing has happened? Yes, I understand when looked at through your world view it may seem trivial or non-existent but now consider how it appears to me? I have explained above what criticism does to my kind and me. It is potentially fatal and sets in motion a series of events, which if not arrested will result in the collapse of my construct, the emergence of the creature and my consigning to oblivion. If you were faced with extinction would you act as if nothing has happened? No you would not. You would do something about it. By understanding how criticism affects us, you should now be in a better position to understand why we react as we do. Stop looking at events through your lens and regard them through mine. Do that and you will realise why we must react in the way that we do.

Accordingly, when faced with a criticism which undermines our very sense of self then we sometimes react by using the now ignited fury as a weapon. As I began to explain, this manifests as an explosive eruption. On other occasions, as it did with my mother, it is an ice cold front which is used as a weapon. Both of these manifestations have different forms which you may be familiar with or you should familiarise yourself with.

Explosive

Bullying

Destructiveness

Mania

Threats

Vengeance

Hurtfulness

Bullying is self-explanatory. Destructiveness covers the destruction of joint property (for example a door in the house), other people's property (a road sign) or more often your personal possessions. Mania involves the manifestation of this ignited fury through such activities as driving aggressively and too fast, speaking too quickly and even walking too fast. It may include bolting down food or consuming alcohol in large quantities. All of this is done to intimidate and frighten through causing the ignited fury to manifest in such a fashion. Threats will be issued either in a howling bellow or a malicious whisper but their effects are undeniable. Vengeance involves being over punitive in our reaction, punishing somebody in an entirely disproportionate fashion. This is often demonstrated against those who we hold some kind of authority over (colleagues, children or pupils for example). Hurtfulness involves a range of behaviours such as sexual abuse, physical abuse, breaking confidences, discrimination, labelling and the use of profane language. This explosion of ignited fury is used to cow, browbeat and intimidate and has a number of outcomes which I describe further below.

The alternative to this explosive manifestation is the cold front. This too has various forms.

Cold Front

Selfishness

Not helping

Cold shoulder

Evasiveness

Secretive behaviour

Stealing

Character assassination

I need not expand on what those forms mean.

Whether we manifest this ignited fury as a cold front or an explosion its primary purpose is to enable us to feel immediately powerful. Your criticism of us has wounded us and we must diminish and extinguish the effect of your criticism. The most immediate method of doing so is to lash out and use this now ignited fury as a weapon. By doing this, we feel powerful and this surge in power enables the damage caused by your criticism to be reduced and ultimately eradicated. By shouting at you in frenzy and seeing you back away in fright, we are underlining that we are superior to you and thus our power is reinforced. By threatening to smash your windows and seeing your eyes widen in terror we gain power and your criticism means far less.

I understand in your world that you deal with criticism differently. You respond in different ways such as:-

Not regarding it as a criticism to begin with
Regarding it as constructive criticism (how I laughed when Dr E explained this to me)
Laughing it off
Becoming angry
Ignoring it
Becoming upset

None of those reactions amount to ignited fury. That is why you and I are different. None of those reactions listed above are applicable to me. I am unable to utilise those reactions as they will not protect me from the wounding nature of your criticism.

My fury must ignite and once that has happened I am able to deal with the injury that you have caused to me. I cannot react in any way other than this. You have a range of different options available to you. I do not. By subjecting you to the cold shoulder so that you follow me around apologising and asking what is wrong, I reinforce that I am the powerful one. I demonstrate that it is I who holds the upper hand in our relationship, whatever form that relationship may take. As soon as I am able to see that my natural superiority has been emphasised and highlighted then the power begins to flow. This sensation of feeling powerful immediately reduces the sting of your criticism. It seals the holes that you have punched into the construct and I am able to overcome the moment of danger and vulnerability.

Using this ignited fury as a weapon is our favoured response. This is because it is immediate in the way it addresses our injury. It is swift and effective. It also has other effects which I expand on shortly. Unfortunately, as I have explained above in the examples of using it as a shield and withdrawal, it is not always possible to utilise ignited fury as a weapon because of some other consequence we wish to avoid.

If you find yourself in a situation with your personal narcissist whereby he or she regularly erupts and uses this ignited fury as a weapon irrespective of the situation, then they lack the discipline to make an informed response. Their injury is just as great as mine, it is the same for us all, however, some of us have the discipline and ability to evaluate the situation and make an informed decision as to how we deal with the criticism. We ascertain what has happened and what is likely to happen and decide to apply withdrawal or the shield instead. Not all of my kind has such ability. They will in the majority of cases use it as a weapon. This is because using it as a weapon is our default setting. It is the instantaneous reaction we have to being criticised. Some of us can contain it and choose an alternative response but not all. For those people it must be used as a weapon either through a cold front or more often through an explosive response. I have discussed this with Dr O and she takes the view that this is something which affects the lower-functioning members of our kind. I concur with that view. Their wiring is different and they lack the high function to make those informed choices. Instead, they must remain with the default setting of using ignited fury as a weapon each and every time they suffer criticism. If you recognise this as being the majority response of your narcissist to criticism then you will be used to the blows landing and the plates being smashed up. I daresay that wedding photograph has been re-framed several times.

I explained above that the primary purpose of using ignited fury as a weapon is to make us feel powerful and diminish the effect of your criticism. It also serves other secondary functions.

Control

Manipulation

Gathering fuel

In respect of control the use of ignited fury as a weapon is to cause you to realise that criticising us is not something you should ever do. We react in this fashion to send a clear message to you that it is you who is at fault and you should not have done or said what you did. This is designed to prevent you from criticising us again at some future point. By demonstrating such a savage and violent response to your criticism you have been given due notice that a repeat criticism will unleash a repeat response from us and you would therefore do well to avoid it. Of course this is often difficult for you because our desire to distort your reality means that there are no rules by which you can try and conform and keep us on side. You are controlled into avoiding the obvious criticisms of us but those which you would not regard as criticisms (but when viewed through our world lens clearly are) are almost impossible for you to avoid.

The manipulation arises through making you do what we want. An example might be as follows. I suggest that we go to a bar that evening for a drink. You respond as follows:-

"I would rather not go out for a drink tonight; we have been out the last two evenings."

"Oh I see, you think my suggestion is a bad idea do you?"

(Immediate criticism)

"No not at all, it is just I am feeling a little tired. If you want to go out, why don't you go with your friends?"

"So you don't want to spend time with me, is that it? Find me too boring do you? That's so selfish of you. I took you out the last two nights because you looked upset and I was cheering you up."

(Further criticism)

"What? We went out because your friends invited us; it was nothing to do with cheering me up?

"Are you calling me a liar?"

(Further criticism)

"No, I am just saying that was the reason we went out."

"That is typical of you, you have no regard for the things I do for you, you are so damn selfish. You are tired so you do not want to go out. What about me? Try thinking about someone other than yourself. In fact, I don't even know why I asked, I should be ashamed to be seen with someone like you. Have you seen how much weight you have put on? Jesus, even a couple of your friends, yes your friends, have remarked on it. You are turning into a whale. You should be thankful I even allow you to come with me to places. Not anymore. Sod you."

"Sorry, they said what? Where has this come from? Look just calm down alright?"

"Calm down? Calm down?! You insult me repeatedly and then have the audacity to suggest I calm down. Good God, you are beyond belief at times. Forget it, I will just stay in and do what you want to do again."

"No no, look I am sorry, I wasn't insulting you, look we will go, it is fine, just let me put my make up on. Just please calm down, we will go out."

Thus the eruption of the ignited fury following criticism results in name calling and threats. This makes us feel powerful and addresses the wounding effect of the criticism. Furthermore, it allows us to manipulate you into agreeing to go to the bar after all even though you would rather not. Of course, once we get there we will spend our time flirting with the bar maid in order to gather some fuel from her and to generate a negative emotional reaction from you and that leads us neatly onto the final secondary consequence of our use as ignited fury as a weapon ; the gathering of fuel.

Consider the following:-

Our manifestation	Your response
Shouting	Fear, anger
Cold shoulder	Concern, apology
Selfishness	upset
Mania	Fear, upset
Labelling	Anger upset
Profanity	Annoyance, upset
Evasiveness	Concern, attention

Each form of explosive or cold fronted fury invariably results in some form of emotional response from you, either of a positive or negative nature and this is what, as you doubtless know, provides us with our fuel. Accordingly, if we lash out at you with our fists, we show dominance and feel powerful thus reducing the effect of your wounding criticism. We see you crying in fright and this provides us with fuel. We may use this violence towards you to force you to do something we want and thus manipulate you all against a back drop of control.

Ignited fury as a weapon is what you will see the most of from a narcissist (either in an explosive or a cold front form) since it is our default setting to dealing with criticism, it is the most effective and the one which provides a range of beneficial outcomes to us. Certain situations may preclude its use, although certain of our kind may not be able to prevent its appearance even though there may be an eventual downside to reacting in such a fashion. Its use is repeated because it is so effective. Its use is repeated because unless we can withdraw or shield (and have the discipline to do so) it is the only response that is afforded to us to deal with your wounding criticism.

Why are we always in a state of fury?

I have written above about how my kind and I have a near permanent state of fury. It is always burning and churning away beneath the surface ready to be ignited at a moment's criticism. This fury has to be there, ready and able to be ignited, because fi it is not we do not have our defence mechanism instantly available to enable us to address your wounding criticism. It is akin to keeping a pan of soup always simmering on your stove just in case somebody drops by and wishes to eat. We must always have this simmering fury available, ready to call on and ignite in defence of ourselves.

Since you now understand why we use fury as we do and you also understand how it is ignited you will appreciate the need for this supply of fury to be on hand at all times, since criticism may come sudden and unexpected. How is it therefore that this fury is always present with us, just lurking beneath the surface and ready to ignite into a weapon or shield?

At first I had no idea as to why I always felt this fury. I knew I felt it. From when I woke until the time I closed my eyes I felt this burning sensation inside. There was this sense of a great amount of energy that was just waiting to be unleashed but I had no idea what was causing it. Through my teenage years I remember experiencing this sensation and how it accompanied me every day. I explain a little later in this chapter how the simmering fury can manifest itself with our kind. Some of us manage to keep it hidden and under wraps until it is needed as ignited fury and then all hell breaks loose. Others of our kind experience a kind of restlessness (that is what I know experience with it) and others struggle to keep the fury concealed and always looks as if they are about to explode. I belonged to this latter category when I was younger. I lacked the discipline (although I later acquired it) to ensure that this simmering fury was concealed from the outside world. I stormed around unable to keep what was churning inside from being seen. During my school days I would snap and lash out at people with scathing words and occasionally a fight. I did not know what it was that made me feel so furious all the time. My father put it down to being a troublesome teenager and that it was just part of growing up.

"Teenagers always behave as malcontents. They struggle to understand their role in the world. They no longer need to be mollycoddled like babies and toddlers, yet they lack the direction and self-sufficiency to place their mark on their world. They are caught between two places and belong to neither."

I remember him explaining this to a doctor when my mother hauled me to see one in order to try and find a reason for this seemingly permanently raging young man. Of course she would not accept any culpability on her part. Not at all. She wanted me to be subjected to all manner of examinations and tests. It was my father, the usual voice of reason, who managed to placate her concerns. I knew she was not concerned as to how I felt. What worried her more was how others would judge her for having a "troublesome and out of control son" as I often heard her complain to my father. Ordinarily my mother would have argued her position until I was trussed up with wires dangling from me but my father relied on his position as a headmaster and his undeniable experience of shepherding thousands of teenage boys into early adulthood to explain why I was as I was. For once my mother listened to him. She was probably just grateful for an explanation and for one that did not stain her parenting in anyway. When I occasionally recall those teenage years (usually at the behest of Drs E and O as I am not prone to nostalgic reminisces myself) I wonder if my father had an idea of what I was because he knew what my mother was. He adored my mother, no matter how awful and difficult she was and I knew he never wanted to be parted from her. Accordingly, I saw how he accommodated her behaviour (which of course planted in my mind how I might use such behaviours to my own benefit) in order to try and lead a quieter life. I suspect he knew what I was as well but in the same way he adopted a non-confrontational style with my mother in order to get through life, he chose to do the same with me and certainly as a teenager he chose to attribute my behaviour to "just being a teenager" rather than something else.

Thus I continued to wear my fury on my sleeve as I moved through my teenage years and this fury regularly ignited when some halfwit criticised me. Nobody was spared my ignited fury and back then I always used it as a weapon. In my discussions with the doctors, I believe that since I lacked awareness then of what I was, I was unable to exert the control over my fury and behaviour so that it was an instantaneous reaction. The fury caught light and next moment someone was subjected to a withering put down or I had put them down on their backside after an assault with my fists. It really was as if some raging beast was inside me and it would be unleashed when I was criticised. I did back then recognise that I hated being criticised although I did not know precisely why. I just felt weakened when somebody did not and offended. Yes, I felt offended that they had the temerity to criticise someone as capable and brilliant as me. I always attributed it to jealousy with my teachers. They were of some excellence but not true brilliance. Those that can, do and those that can't teach and all that. I knew they felt a resentment towards me because they realised I was destined for better and greater things than them. I imagined they once had high hopes of being pioneers, leaders and captains of industry but those hopes had been dashed on the rocks of disappointment and they found themselves stuck in a rut. Year after year they trotted out the same lessons to pupils, a number of whom who would exceed what those teachers could ever do and that reminded them of their own failings. With someone as able as me they could not help but try and put me down with their criticisms, all of which were unfounded and all of which ignited my fury, leading me to regular dressing downs by them, occasional exclusion from the class and the odd caning. I took it in my stride because I knew when I let out this fury I always felt better. As soon as I had retorted to that teacher or a fellow pupil using my acerbic wit to put them in their place that I instantly felt improved and powerful. Yes my caustic response might lead to me being dragged from the classroom by my sideburn or taking a punch from an older boy but back then I did not care for the consequence of my actions. All I knew was that by letting this fury out I would feel better and the sting of the criticism would just fade away. Older and wiser I understand now why this is the case. I am able to look back and see how I allowed the fury to ignite and how I had used it as a weapon to assert my superiority and reduce and then extinguish the effect of the criticism that had been levelled at me.

It was not too long before I realised that more severe consequences than detention and a good talking to would follow if I allowed by ignited fury to be used in this way. This meant that I developed other strategies to utilise this ignited fury. Occasionally I would exit from the source of the criticism and content myself with the knowledge that the critical comment would be a distant memory and I had asserted my higher status by being able to evade further hurtful comments. I also realised that I could protect myself from the criticisms even when I was unable to exit or chose not to lash out at my critics. I at first found this arduous and it would invariably mean I would need some form of affirmation and support from an alternative source. I know realise that I was seeking fuel to replenish my depleted power in creating my shield. At the time I just knew I could protect myself but I always needed some reassurance and admiration from elsewhere and I needed to find it promptly.

I became more aware of how criticism wounded me and even more aware of how I could negate its effects by using my ignited fury, what I did not understand though was where this fury came from and why it was always there. As a teenager it had always been there and I was hardly able to conceal its presence. With maturity came the ability to mask it. As I honed my manipulative abilities I recognised the value in presenting a particular face to the world. A face which was seductive, acceptable and attractive and this meant keeping the simmering fury hidden away from view until it were needed. I became adept at doing this and almost all of those who came into my world never saw what was brewing beneath that wide smile and sparkling eyes. Those that spent more time with me saw the restlessness but they were not able to attribute that to what it actually was.

I covered the simmering fury and I knew how to use my ignited fury, but it took a number of years before I began to realise what it was that created this simmering fury in the first place. I struggle to recall precisely when I gained some insight into what it was that made me feel permanently on the edge of frenzy. What I do remember is that my first realisation was based on feeling that the whole world was against me because of who I was and how that was utterly unfair. It stood in judgement against me and it had no standing to do so. I did not feel sorry for myself at this unjust state of affairs although I had every right to do so. No, instead I felt furious. How dare the world treat me in this manner? Why should it behave in such a way towards someone who was of an elevated position, who was superior and able? That was unfair and wrong. I was preoccupied with this notion. I would wake and look across at the person sleeping next to me and immediately I would think that she would most likely be judging me in some way. What gave her the right to do this? She had no such right yet it still happened. Instantly the simmering fury would be there as I pushed back the bedclothes and rose from the bed. I would wash, dress and eat breakfast before heading off for my first lecture. As I walked through the streets, surrounded by the beautiful and historical buildings I passed my fellow undergraduates who no doubt would be passing judgement on me. Again I raged against this. Did they now know who I was and what I was capable of? The fury continued. Sat in the first tutorial I would stare at my tutor as his eyes flicked across my latest paper and there was the fury once again as I waited for his comment. Another who was sat in judgement and on what basis? Years of hiding in his ivory tower? What did he really know about my excellence? Thus this was how I first realised the basis on which my ever present fury was based. The world was judging me and it was biased against me.

This knowledge increased as my years did. My awareness of what was generating this unceasing fury increased. With the assistance of Dr E and Dr O I have been able to touch on even further reasons why this fury is generated. Sometimes I knew as the realisation arose from a particular situation. I recall gaining awareness of this when I first entered the world of work and a colleague failed to deliver on what he had promised and made me look poor into the bargain. His failure to live up to the expected excellence which he had conned me (how dare he do so) into believing he could deliver made me feel furious and I again chalked up another reason to add to the growing list of the instances which generated my fury. In other cases it has been through discussion and analysis with Dr E and Dr O that the awareness has increased. Occasionally they have suggested a basis for this fury and on reflection I have agreed with what has been put forward, on many occasions I have not. Sometimes I will be describing a particular scenario or instance and from my words and experiences they have plucked another causative factor for my fury.

This fury is ever present because we are always furious with the world around us. Thus fury arises for several different reasons and through the journey and work I have undertaken as I have described above, I am able now to relay to you what the causative factors are that generate this ever present simmering fury.

1. Our fury at how harshly the world has treated us;
2. Our fury at having to seek fuel each and every day or face obliteration;
3. Our fury at the injustice of our situation. Why someone should as great as us be subjected to the repeated attempts to cast us down and belittle us?
4. Our fury at people not paying us the attention and admiration that we deserve;

5. Our fury at people repeatedly letting us down after all we have invested in them, by not providing us with the fuel we deserve and demand;

6. Our fury at people not reaching our expectations;

7. Our fury at the loneliness of being above so many people, being this special is both a blessing and a curse;

8. Our fury at having to keep the construct in place in order to generate more fuel;

9. Our fury at having to keep the construct in place in order to imprison the creature;

10. Our fury at having this creature waiting to consign us to oblivion should it escape;

11. Our fury at being judged by people who have no standing or authority to do so;

12. Our fury at people expecting us to speak, think and behave in accordance with their world view when ours is vastly different.

It is possible there are others which I have not identified or it may be that further factors present themselves and "grow" which are yet to be added to this list.

All of this unfairness and injustice is felt by us every single day and this engenders a fury inside us. A simmering fury at you, your family, our family, our friends, our colleagues, the man next door and the lady in the supermarket. A fury at the world. The world has created us this way and we are forced to deal with it as best we can by our unceasing search for fuel and the demonstration of our brilliance to those around us. It is a burden that we must carry and we are filled with this fury at all times.

It is often only those who are closest to our kind who see this simmering fury since we prefer to maintain a façade of perfection and success to everybody else. Those who are frequently subjected to the ignited fury come to recognise that this fury is always burning away. It manifests in a restlessness that we exhibit. We may never be able to sit still, or watch one television programme as we flit from channel to channel. I remember one of my former girlfriends likening me to a caged beast.

"You seem to pad around the house all the time, unable to relax, as if you are waiting to spring on someone. You are like a caged beast." She once remarked. Her description is apt. We carry this fury with us all the time and it may cause us to act in a restless fashion as we seek some distraction from the fury within. In my case the fury is ever present but I am able to keep it below the surface and it will only manifest when it is ignited through somebody's criticism of me. The rest of the time I am able to conceal it to the world at large by maintaining my carefully constructed façade of all round good guy. With those who spend more time with me, such as family or an intimate partner, it is harder to maintain such a façade so the simmering fury remains well-hidden. In those instances it does manifest as the restlessness that I have described. In others of my kind, they are less able to keep the fury hidden. Their fury has not yet been ignited but its potency is such that keeping it concealed proves difficult for them and the raging, churning fury is only kept in check by the thinnest of veneers. This barrier is so slender it is almost transparent and in those instances the relevant person is seen as a simmering volcano just waiting to explode. Such a person appears permanently on the edge of explosion, their mannerisms, facial expressions and actions all denote an individual who will blow up in an instant. You will be able to see the fire blazing in his or her eyes, the furrowed brow, the clenched fists and the walk. The walk is one of a ferocious giant which clomps and stamps its way around through home, shopping mall and workplace. If this person was a cartoon character their face would be red and perspiring, steam would be expelled from his ears and his body would be bulging and knotted. Those of our kind who have the thinnest of barriers are visible pressure cookers. Our fury makes us all pressure cookers but those of us who are unable to keep the fury hidden until it is ignited really do appear like they will blow any second.

I have understood from my work with the doctors that much of this is regarded as my perception of the world. That may be correct but nevertheless it is my perception. It is not a thing that should be regarded as a good thing or a bad thing, it just is and I am the one who has to deal with it. This reality (or perception if you follow the doctors' line of thinking) is what I have to deal with each and every day and that is why the fury is always there.

I can feel the fury now as I write. It is always there. The sensation is just under the surface waiting to be called on. Sometimes it ebbs a little, perhaps when I am more relaxed or distracted, but it never seems to vanish in its entirety. I feel it surge and swell as it grows, brimming with the potency that is waiting to be ignited and unleashed against those that offend me. The fury is as much a part of me as your desire to empathise and care is a part of you. You cannot strip it from me. Even when I appear relaxed that fury is still there. I may look relaxed lying on a sun lounger, soaking up the summer sunshine as I listen to some music but do not be misled. The fury is never far away. Think about the times when you have been subjected to your narcissist's fury. Does it seem as if it has come out of nowhere? Does it appear without warning as you are subjected to a ferocious rage attack? Are you left perplexed as to what even caused it? The answer is that the simmering fury was just ready to be ignited and unleashed. We are like volcanoes. We have a mass of searing hot lava inside us and a very brittle crust that is just keeping this torrent of lava in check. Your criticism will penetrate this crust in an instant and thus the pressurised lava will erupt in a devastating display and shower you with the super-heated lava.

It is the way of this world, the way it has treated my kind and me and continues to do so, especially through people like you, that has created this simmering and ever present fury. It is you and those like you who criticise us and thus ignite this fury so that it is unleashed in all of its ferocious glory. It may recede for a short while, especially if we have to convert it into power to make us feel powerful and shield ourselves. It may ebb when something or somebody has distracted us from the cruel world we have been forced to inhabit, but what it does not do is disappear. Ever.

The Effect Our Fury Has On You

I have explained above how using fuel as a weapon has certain secondary consequences through control, manipulation and fuel. Those are of course consequences which arise to our benefit although they naturally affect you. Since they benefit me then I am aware of them and embrace them. How does our fury make you feel? I can see how it makes you feel. I see the tears, the anger, the fear and the dejection. I feed on those emotional reactions of yours and need them. I am of course unable to ascertain truly how you feel because as you will know by now I have been stripped of any capacity to empathise as it serves no purpose for me. Nevertheless, in order to provide some balance and at the urging of the good doctors I thought I would let you read some of the comments from those who have been subjected to my ignited fury. I daresay some of these admissions and recollections will resonate with your own experiences.

"I was terrified of your rages. I tried to work out what caused them but they seemed to come out of nowhere and for the strangest of reasons. I just wanted to curl into a ball and hope for the best until it blew over."

"I would die inside when I knew the iciness would begin. I could not ascertain what would cause it to happen but I knew it was on its way as soon as I saw that look in your eye. It was as if your eyes had iced over and I knew then that you would ignore me for days on end. The only acknowledgement I would ever get was a cold, damning stare which seemed to be willing me to die. I can even feel that horrible sensation inside as I write this down. Nobody has ever made me feel as if I were absolutely nothing in the way you did. I am glad it hasn't happened again, part of me died every time you did it to me."

"I was left always on edge by your temper. I only had to say or do the wrong thing and then I would be on the receiving end of it and Jesus it was horrible. After a while I realised I moved anything breakable that I valued and put it somewhere else because you always made a bee-line for those things when your temper erupted. You never laid a hand on me although I always thought that would change when you used to fly off the handle. It was frightening and I realised it left me on edge and anxious."

"I was always fiercely proud of my independence and resilience until I met you and your temper. You always knew what to say to have me in floods of tears. No matter how much I apologised and I did not even know half the time what I was apologising about, you never relented. You could see how upset I was and I swear you revelled in it. You made me hurt, upset and miserable each time you lashed out at me. It was so horrible."

"It was the bangs that I came to dread. I worked it out after I left for the third time that you had found out that I hated my dad banging when he was angry, when I was a child. You got that information from me and you used it against me. When you went into a rage you never hit me, you never broke anything and you never even shouted at me. All you ever did was bang things. You would shut doors with a bang, slam books on the table, stamp your foot on the wooden floor or crash the over door or dishwasher door shut. Each time you would move around bang, bang and bang. I would stand there screaming at you to stop with my hands over my ears and tears down my face but you carried on. You knew exactly what to do. It is years since I was with you but I still jump whenever there is a sudden noise. That's you and my father I have to thank for that. Two of a kind you are."

"It was being frozen out by you that upset me the most. If I offended you in some way at work then that would be it. Down would come the shutters, the doors would be bricked up and I would be excluded. You would not speak to me, you would not invite me for team drinks, you would not even include me in group e-mails. It was horrible and what made it even worse was that when I complained about you to your boss I was told to stop telling-tales and just to get on with it. After two years of this happening to me on and off I had had enough and I left. I am pleased to say I work somewhere which does not have a resident wanker like you."

"You made me a shell. I walked on those eggshells as I waited for the inevitable dressing down. No physical violence, no you are too clever for that, but it was the tirades. I always knew you were good with words. It was one of the things that attracted me to you in the first place and if I am honest I realise now how you used your skill with words to seduce me and I loved it. I still miss it to be truthful. But by God how you could turn those sweet words into weapons. You never swore much though. I always found that odd, it was strange, it was like I was being politely assaulted but in some ways that was worse than being hit by a thug. I used to cower as you rained those nasty tirades down on me, that beautiful mouth spewing such awful words at me, berating and belittling me. Bruises heal but the verbal battering you gave me still goes around in my head today."

"You have the nastiest temper I have ever experienced. I hope you die soon you bastard."

"I tried so hard to understand what it was that made you seem like you were at war with the world. Even the most banal of comments seemed to set you off. I got the impression you were always angry, permanently angry and the slightest thing would set you off. I was frightened of you even though I loved you and wanted to try and help you, but no matter what I did, it never worked. I am sorry I failed. Perhaps someone better might be able to help you."

"I was so taken aback the first time you put me down that I thought you were talking to someone else. You were sly about it though. You always did it when nobody was paying attention. It was often little more than a sentence but you would have me in pieces and running to the bathroom to cry and try to pull myself together. I don't really know how you managed to have this effect on me. I think it was because I loved you so much, more than anyone I have ever loved. I miss you still even though I know I am better off without you and your savage put-downs."

"When we hung out together if someone got on your nerves you would just cut them dead. You always seemed to know exactly how to hurt them the most with just a few words. I remember Tom running off crying and he was eighteen. You made him look like a baby. We were in awe of you, well that and frightened of you as we did not want to be next."

"John and Belinda always referred to you as departure lounge because when you stayed there if someone said something you did not like you just walked off. No matter what you were doing you would just up sticks and disappear."

"We approached our appraisals with a mixture of anticipation and dread. If we had pleased you we benefitted from your generosity and your influence. There was no doubt about it. If we dared challenged anything you said then blimey, you would take us down and we knew we were in trouble then. I realise you were only doing it to make us try harder and be better at our jobs but it was never pleasant being on the receiving end of one of your roastings. It only happened to me the once I am pleased to say. Once was one time too many."

An interesting array of reactions. Not everyone asked responded and I guess they must have their own reasons. It is fascinating how the use of our ignited temper affects people and there is just a snapshot of the way it affected people I was involved in from girlfriends, to friends, colleagues and family members. I have purposefully not included names or how I know these people to allow you to guess what our connection was. Some are more obvious than others. Of course, what all of these people had in common was the fact that they had criticised me in some form. If they had not done this most heinous act then they would not have ignited the simmering fuel and be subjected to the appropriate manifestation of this potent instrument.

I am aware of the long-term effects of being subjected to our fury, from my reading of other works. I have read about the impact it has on somebody being subjected to seemingly random eruptions of fury which do not appear to be based on anything substantial. I have read of the consequences for those who experience a daily diet of shouting or insults, the aggregated effect of being frozen out over seemingly nothing and the combination of belittlement and denigration over time. It is not my place to go into the detail of those effects since although our behaviour causes them, I am not privy to how these effects come about. That is better left to others to discuss. Moreover, it is not the point of this book to detail those consequences. This book is focussed on allowing you to understand what our fury is, why it ignites and how it manifests.

Dealing With Our Fury

Thus I have explained to you what our fury is, how it is created and how it is ever present. I have explained what causes it be ignited and then how this ignited fury manifests. I have detailed how this manifestation of ignited fury is used and what purposes it serves for us. This naturally provides you with a far better understanding of our fury but leads to the inevitable question of how might you deal with out fury.

Dealing with our fury presents several options:

1. Implementing No Contact to escape us entirely;
2. Avoiding igniting our fury and the consequence that flow from doing so; or
3. Managing the consequences that flow from ignited fury.

No Contact

As with everything to do with our kind implementing No Contact is the holy grail of tackling us and that is also addressed in **Escape** alongwith some very useful preparatory observations in **Departure Imminent.** In order to avoid duplication I will not go into the detail of those publications here but rather direct you to consider their content as part of your methodology of dealing with our fury.

Avoiding Igniting the Fury

You may have considered that in addressing the question of not igniting the fury, how about getting rid of the fury in the first place. I am afraid that is an impossible task. You might be able to reduce the simmering fury by relaxing us and distracting us but you will not be able to do this at all times and it does not ever totally remove the simmering fury and therefore you would need to question whether you regard it as worthwhile applying your energy in this fashion.

Do not think that you ever get rid of the fury. I have explained that this simmering fury is ever present and I have detailed the reasons why this is. In order to eradicate this simmering fury you would need to tackle all of the injustices this world applies to our kind. Such an undertaking is beyond even the most golden-hearted of empathic individuals. Dr E and Dr O have made mention of how many of the causative factors that bring about this simmering fury are based on our perceptions of how the world is and how it treats us. I understand people view the world in differing ways but there are reasons why that is so. I view it in my way because that is how it is. You view it in a different way in order to try and deal with the world the best you can. It is a laudable notion, I will give you that. Dr E and Dr O have made gentle noises about altering those perceptions but I have rejected those suggestions. I see the world how it truly is. That is the consequence of my brilliance. Others look at it through rose-tinted spectacles for whatever reason it serves for them. I do not. I see it as exactly how it is and whilst I understand that you and your kind, including the good doctors, base their attempts to shift my way of thinking and doing by attributing it to perception, I know that it is just a ruse. Accordingly, there is no hope to alter the causative factors that create our simmering fury.

The most obvious step you can take is to avoid igniting this simmering fury. Do not criticise us and we have no basis for ignition and thus there is no basis for a manifestation of this ignited fury. Consider carefully what you will say to us or what you will do beforehand. Create a filter for your words and behaviour and remove anything that criticises us, no matter how minor or trivial you may regard it. You need to regard your comments not from your point of view but from ours. I know you are very good at putting yourself into the shoes of others and therefore considering how we would regard your remark or gesture (especially now you have read the contents of this book) will enable you to weed out much that causes us offence. You tell us often how much you love us. Prove it and create this filter and remove the criticism. You will benefit from this for without criticism we need not ignite the fury. It will just churn away beneath the surface but will not be unleashed and as you know from experience and the comments above, the unleashing of the ignited fuel is best avoided.

I cannot guarantee you will catch all of your critical words and actions. I am aware from what has been said to me that you regard our reactions as being based on trivial comments or even non-existent events. That is not the case, not from our point of view. By extending yourself and considering how we might regard a certain comment or gesture you will soon realise how it is wounding to us even if it is not wounding to you. By doing this you should be able to ensure you avoid most, maybe even all, criticisms of us and therefore you will avoid igniting the fuel and the consequences that follow from that. If there is anything that can protect you from the manifestation of out ignited fuel it is avoiding criticising us. I recognise from comments made that you may regard this as unfair and arduous but then that is what we face with the world being the way it is. If you are unable to implement No Contact and find you must remain in contact with the narcissist in your life in some shape or form then two options remain open to you.

1. Reduce and avoid any criticism of us. This will prevent the ignition of our fury;
2. Manage the manifestation of the ignited fury.

I have dealt with item one already, what about item two?

Managing the Manifestation of Ignited Fury

Some of the manifestations of our ignited fury have been discussed in my books **Manipulated** and **Escape:How to Beat the Narcissist**. In order to avoid duplication I would suggest you have regard to the content of those publications, if you have not done so already, for further information on how to manage those particular manifestations of our ignited fury such as intimidation or character assassination.

A further method open to you is to harness the power of withdrawal. I have explained above that withdrawal is one of our options when we have been wounded with criticism. Sometimes it is not an option for us because of the situation that we find ourselves in. If you have tried to reduce the instances by which the fuel can be ignited then this will afford you additional strength and energy to apply to finding a method by which we can withdraw. If you are able to facilitate our withdrawal we will take that and remove ourselves to enable the wound from your criticism to heal. You will also now know why we walk away and you will not make the mistake of following us and pressing for answers whereby you are adding to the criticism and wounding and therefore running the risk of us having to use our ignited fuel as a weapon against you. Once you realise that we have reacted to your criticism then it is not too late to offer us as way out. The simplest way to do this would be to state:

"I have upset you. I am sorry. I did not mean to do so. I am going to leave you alone for a short while. I apologise."

Not only have you given us some fuel but you have immediately reinforced our superiority by recognising your error almost straight away. By withdrawing you are not making anything of our need to be alone and heal our wound. In fact this subservient act will please us as it underlines our standing over you. I would caution that this may not always work. There are two reasons for this.

1. Your narcissist is of a low-functioning variety and therefore instantly erupts with ignited fury as a weapon. It will be difficult to manage that but not impossible.

2. Your criticism may have wounded significantly so that we feel we have no option other than to go on the attack and use our ignited fuel as a weapon.

Notwithstanding these risks, looking to utilise withdrawal as a method of diminishing the effect of ignited fury. In a social setting you should be able to recognise when the affront has taken place, even if not caused by you and in such a scenario you may consider moving yourself and your narcissist away from the source of the criticism. By you making the suggestion of heading to the bar, we do not feel belittled by having to move away from the source since it it at your suggestion and not at ours. We do not feel our withdrawal will invite ridicule or scorn in such a circumstance. Accordingly, withdrawal is a very useful strategy for you to deploy in assisting yourself and also us in taking the least disruptive response to when we have been criticised and the fury has been ignited.

You should also ensure that if the fury has been ignited that you do not exacerbate it in anyway by decrying our reaction. This will just make it worse and in certain instances may cause a lesser reaction (such a withdrawal or shield) to blow up into the ignited fuel being used as a weapon.

If you are not able to implement No Contact then you can reduce the risk of igniting the fury by filtering your comments and behaviour to remove criticisms. Those that do still strike us and ignite the fuel will be much reduced and you can then seek to manage those through a combination of securing withdrawal, avoidance of exacerbation and the techniques outlined in **Escape.**

Conclusion

This book should now have provided you with a greater understanding of fury and its application to and relationship with the narcissist. Fury is not anger. Anger is a normal reaction. Fury is more than anger; it is on a greater scale and is an abnormal response. Fury is an applicable response to various categories of disordered individuals and especially to the narcissist. The narcissist always possesses fury because:-

1. Of the way the world treats us; and
2. We use fury as an instrument

Criticism is the enemy of the narcissist. It wounds our kind and threatens to demolish our construct which will cease our existence. Criticism also ignites our fury. Criticism is the very thing that can lead to our destruction but it is also the catalyst for the means by which we can preserve our existence. The ignition of our fury allows us to manifest this ever present state in an aggressive or passive-aggressive fashion. Criticism may cause our withdrawal where this is a viable option, to enable us to avoid further criticism and to allow us to recuperate and repair the construct. Where withdrawal does not occur then the ignited fury is used either as a shield to allow the construct to be repaired. The ignited fury uses up power which depletes our fuel which must then be replaced. Alternatively, the ignited fury is used as a weapon by which more fuel can be gathered (which diminishes the wounding effect of the criticism by reinforcing our might, importance and superiority) and allows us to use this ignited fury as a weapon to control and manipulate.

The repeated manifestation of the ignited fury is necessary to preserve our existence and repair or override the wounding effect of criticism. If we did not ignite the fury then we would cease to exist. Accordingly, the ever present fury must be ignited to enable us to survive. This means that you and others will be repeatedly subjected to this fury with all of the attendant downsides that arise from this. Sustained exposure to our ignited fury is not only most unpleasant for you it has further consequences and effects on your well-being.

Fury always stays with the narcissist. Ignited fury must exist to counter the wounding effects of criticism. Should there be no criticism then the fury remains but it is not ignited and thus the consequences of this ignited fury can be avoided. Of course, in our reality which is different from yours, we perceive more things as criticisms and thus there are far more catalysts for us to be wounded and for the fury to be ignited. That is what makes being in close proximity to a narcissist such an anxious existence. The slightest look or comment will be perceived as a wounding criticism and the ever present fury is ignited.

We use our ignited fury to protect ourselves but in so doing we invariably affect you by controlling, manipulating and provoking an emotional reaction which in turn provides us with fuel. The consequences of being subjected to our ignited fury can be devastating for you. We cannot stop the ignition of this fury. It must be done to deal with the horrendous consequences of your criticism of us. You may find ways of reducing or avoiding the effect of being subjected to our ignited fury, but for us the simmering fury will always be there and with that there is always the risk of its ignition and the consequences that follow from that.

Our fury is ever present and is absolute. Now you know why. Thank you for reading.

Further reading by H G Tudor

Evil

Narcissist: Seduction

Narcissist: Ensnared

Manipulated

Confessions of a Narcissist

More Confessions of a Narcissist

Further Confessions of a Narcissist

From the Mouth of a Narcissist

Escape: How to Beat the Narcissist

Danger: 50 Things You Should Not Do With a Narcissist

Departure Imminent: Preparing for No Contact to beat the Narcissist

Fuel

Chained: The Narcissist's Co-Dependent

A Delinquent Mind

All available on Amazon

Further interaction with H G Tudor

Knowing the Narcissist

@narcissist_me

Facebook

Narcsite.wordpress.com

Made in the USA
Middletown, DE
16 September 2020